The Magic of Parenting

Lessons from the Danish Way of Parenting, the Happiest People in the World

A. Lawton

GIVING TREE PRESS

ISBN 978-1-965145-02-9

Published by Giving Tree Press PB

support@lapublishings.com

To Peter and Adelaide!

You two are the most wonderful, unique, creative individuals I know. Our hearts are full of gratitude to be your parents, and to have the deep relationship and traditions that make up our family. You two have been my inspiration and my reason to do many things and make changes in my life. I have loved watching you grow and learn through such difficulties and joy in our life together. You two are the miracles your dad and I prayed for and we want you to know you are always and forever loved!!

Acknowledgements

I am extremely grateful to the many adults in my life who have spent time, tears, love, and direction on this journey through parenting. There are many who have touched my life and as I wrote this book a few really stood out to me, who I would like to acknowledge at this time. To Renaun and Eve, I want to express my sincere gratitude for supporting me on this parenting journey, teaching me by example and through educational resources. To Kaer and Ryan, my many thanks to them for including me in their home and family through out my life. To JoAnn, the mother of my oldest and dearest friend, I am grateful for the opportunities she gave me to learn about childcare in my youth. Her mentorship and support have had a lasting impact on my life. I am eternally grateful for my parents, Kathleen and Ranel, who gave me life. I would like to thank them for raising us eight children to the best of their ability. Their love, prayers, and unwavering support have always been a source of strength for me. Now to my sweet husband, Loren, who has been there through all the parenting ups and downs. With deepest gratitude in my heart, thank you for giving and living this life with me!! Thank you all from the deepest part of me, I have been changed by you. Last but certainly not least, I thank God for His infinite mercy and grace. For His wisdom, guidance and trust in me through this parenting journey!

Contents

Introduction   1

The Journey to Authentic Parenting   4

Exploring Danish Parenting   9

Let's Talk About Hygge   31

Friluftsliv and Lagom   40

Playtime Brings Life Growth and Overall Good Health   48

Parenting Begins With You   60

How a Child's Brain Works   74

Mental Health for the Whole Family   87

Living the Danish Way of Parenting   100

Conclusion   115

Glossary   119

References   121

The Wandering Lawtons   128

More Books From the Publisher   130

Introduction

Raising children has always been my dream, but little did I know how transformative the journey would be—not just for my kids, but for me as well. Even though I know this journey is ever evolving, I find myself with the desire to share what I have experienced and discovered. There have been times when others have asked me about my parenting methods and I am always thrilled to share it with them. I feel every child should have the chance at a mom and dad who will love and guide them to the best of their abilities at that time. We know that raising our children does not come with a manual, but what if there was a philosophy that could bring more calm and connection into your home? I found that the Danish way of parenting with a mix of other methods, created a sense of magic for our family. Through trial, error, observation and research, I've discovered a style of parenting that feels right for us and I believe that what I have written will help many other families. I will do my best to describe the knowledge and lessons in a way you can blend it into your own life and family. As it's a blend of empathy, authenticity, fresh air playtime, no ultimatums, encouraging autonomy, independence, respect, and a lot of togetherness, *hygge,* *(pronounced* (**hyoo**·guh),—the Danish concept of warmth and coziness—which is why I decided to write this book: *The Magic of Parenting: Lessons from the Danish Way of Parenting, the Happiest People in the World.*

When I was a child I was given the opportunity to tag along with my sisters in their babysitting jobs. I loved it so much I babysat all through my teen years and went into university to pursue early childhood education, where I eagerly learned about child development and behavior. I couldn't wait to be a mother. When I became a mom of two lovely children my preparation was going to be put to the test. But nothing could have fully prepared me for the reality of becoming a mother. I learned that no amount of preparation could have predicted the emotional complexity of raising children. It was through sleepless nights, toddler tantrums, deep desires for their well being and the endless need for patience that I truly realized just how hard—and rewarding—this journey would be.

Parenthood can be a journey filled with joy, love, and growth, but it can also be filled with frustration, doubt, and confusion. You set out on your parenting journey with the best intentions. You've been given advice, but it doesn't take long to realize that even words of wisdom from well-meaning friends will not make this trip any easier. You are in uncharted lands, and your path is littered with detours and dead ends.

There were many wonderful experiences in my childhood, however I also knew I wanted to change a few things about how I was raised. I wanted to avoid the anger, yelling, uninvolvement, discipline, and dismissing emotions. While I had strong ideas about the kind of mother I wanted to be, I had to figure out how to put those ideas into practice. Through my own experience and years of research, I found that the Danish approach to parenting aligned perfectly with the kind of parent I wanted to be. Danish parents focus on empathy, communication, respect and a strong emotional connection with their children, which fosters resilience and independence in them. This parenting style offers a nurturing, warm environment where children can thrive as individuals, and it also provides structure and expectations that help them understand their role in the family and in society.

This book is not about creating perfect children—because that's unrealistic—but about helping you create a home where your children feel loved, heard, and supported. I want to share the methods and resources I've picked up, not just from my research into Danish parenting, but from my own journey as a mother. These strategies have transformed the way I parent, and I hope they will help you build stronger family bonds, improve communication, and raise resilient, independent children.

As you read through this book, I'll guide you through the lessons I've learned and introduce you to the core concepts of Danish parenting. You'll find practical ideas for incorporating free play, family traditions, and open communication into your home. My goal is to help you create an environment where your children can thrive emotionally, socially, and intellectually. Together, we can explore a parenting style that emphasizes empathy, connection, and joy—a style that will not only benefit your children but your entire family.

Let's embark on this journey together. After all, parenting truly is magical, and I can't wait to share that bit of magic with you.

The Journey to Authentic Parenting

This book won't offer a one-size-fits-all formula, but it will provide you with insights, methods and philosophies that helped transform our family, which I think will benefit your family too. I think you will also come to see how the Danish way of parenting is done with authenticity. This authentic parenting is seeing your child as a person not someone to be controlled, manipulated, victimized or coerced.

I grew up in a family of eight, with parents who both worked in education, which fostered my love of learning about child development, leadership and family life. There were unfortunately many of the above stated in our family dynamic. I developed a curiosity about the dynamics of other families, whether they were similar or different from mine. Learning how different families interacted with one another and with life came from reading books, living with other families, classes, talking with others as well as my travels and nomadic living all over the world. Ultimately, I focused on the Danish parenting style. I'm impressed with how Danish society lives, how parents interact with their kids and their overall approach to parenting.

Like many parents, I entered this journey with high ideals. I promised myself I wouldn't yell, spank, or belittle my children's emotions. I wanted to foster a home where they felt heard and understood, where communication would always be open, and empathy would guide our interactions. But the realities of parenthood quickly tested those promises. There were moments when my patience was stretched thin, when my children's defiance or frustration mirrored my own. There were times when my childhood instincts kicked in, and I found myself defaulting to the very approaches I swore I wouldn't use.

We've all experienced the days of our little ones yelling "NO" to even the most reasonable question. Adorable toddlers become tiny rage monsters when the world does not go their way. We give our little humans a task that we believe will help them learn responsibility, and they reward us by muttering "I don't want to" followed by "I hate you" in response.

Often we're too close to the situation to recognize what is happening, but through all the drama and chaos, our children are learning and growing. We sometimes forget, even when we are at our worst, our children are like sponges soaking everything up. We are their road map for life, so they watch us and consciously imitate our behaviors. No matter how upset our children get with us, we are still their primary role models. They are exposed to us every day, some all day, and they look to us for guidance, as they grow and learn life lessons.

It didn't take long to see that parenting isn't about perfection—it's about growth. My children, in their most challenging moments, were showing me what they needed: connection, understanding, and space to express themselves. It wasn't about controlling their behavior; it was about recognizing their emotions and guiding them through those feelings with empathy. This realization became a turning point in how I approached parenting.

There was a time when my daughter, who is a head strong, dynamic person, showed her feelings in a rage of words and movement. I noticed she needed some space and a hug, not my angry words or correction. This is just one instance that comes to mind, however there are so many different reactions we and our kids give to our experiences. I found that being in tuned to what my children are feeling, being patient and acting in an empathetic, kind manner helped most in our interactions.

We all know and accept that everybody is different and no two people are exactly alike, yet society is determined to place children in boxes. Ironically, adults are quick to label children, and we quickly attach these labels to our offspring. We conclude that there are shy kids, talented kids, brave kids, athletic kids, bullies and so on. Society says all boys and girls will act in specific ways based on their gender. We also determine that different age groups will all have the same specific behaviors.

I quickly discovered that my preconceptions could make the parenting journey a challenge. I expected my children to be just like me, with similar personalities and traits, so I thought I would know what they needed and our bond would be tight because of our similarities. I loved playing and interacting with children, so I thought it would be a breeze with my own. However, even though that's great and helps, I realized that being close to anyone, even my children, meant that I needed to recognize their uniqueness. Everyone has a distinct personality, and sometimes assuming you know what is best for someone else can present difficulties.

When I started this journey toward the Danish parenting style, my husband was a willing participant, but he was a bit more hesitant. In our culture, the parenting styles we were used to, the women set the tone of the household while the father is the disciplinarian and leaves the daily parenting up to the mother. That meant my husband wasn't sure how to approach this new style.

The Danish approach is quite different from what we knew. There are no strict roles for men or women in their family—something we'll discuss further, later in the book. Danish parents work together as a team, and once my husband saw the benefits of this parenting style, he fully embraced it. Thank goodness, because I couldn't have done this without him! Today, I see him patiently communicating with our children and listening to them in ways that create a sweet atmosphere of respect and trust. We both came from environments where children obeyed their parents out of fear or obligation, often resulting in guilt or shame when they didn't live up to their expectations. But now, within our own family, we've cultivated a home where our children honor us not out of fear, but because they respect and trust us.

When we become parents, it's common for us to promise that we will fix the wrongs our parents did and avoid making the same mistakes. Unfortunately, it's also normal for us to feel parental guilt when the life we so carefully planned goes sideways and we find ourselves slipping into what we know—which is what we were taught or how we were raised. So how do we let go of the habits we learned in childhood and embrace our evolution as parents with a brand-new approach to nurturing?

I believe that is why you are here, reading to gather ideas and education that might be that piece you are looking for. While I knew what I wanted to change, I didn't know how to do it at first. I feel that through trial and error, study and living out what I learned, and seeing this in other families, we have found a parenting rhythm that can feel like a dream at times.

This journey has shown me that parenting is not about control. It's about creating an environment where children feel safe to be themselves and to express their emotions without judgment. It's about fostering independence while offering guidance. It's about listening as much as it is teaching. I've learned that children watch everything we do, and the way we handle their emotions—and our own—becomes the roadmap they follow.

Of course, emotional connection is only one part of the picture. Children need space to grow in other ways as well, and this is where play comes in. **Play is an essential element** of the Danish parenting style because it allows children to develop independence, creativity, and problem-solving skills. It encourages them to explore their world and learn through experience. I will go into much more detail about the importance of play in a later chapter, but for now, it's worth mentioning that play is one of the most natural ways children grow emotionally and socially.

In the next chapter we will explore Danish society and their parenting style. With the following chapters supporting this topic and bits of wisdom and thoughts from my experiences and research. You're probably reading this book because you have heard of this parenting style but aren't sure what it's all about. Or you may be reading this because you want to find bits and pieces of this parenting philosophy to incorporate along with other techniques you have, and that is wonderful. I don't believe there is a right or wrong way to navigate your parenting journey. What works for one family may not work for another, and that's what life is about—finding what fits the dynamic personalities that make up your family culture.

Exploring Danish Parenting

Insights Into What Makes Them the Happiest People in the World

The Danish people earned the title of being called "the happiest in the world" based on a report from the United Nations' World Happiness Day, which takes place on March 20. The resulting report, based on facts such as income and life expectancy, places Denmark consistently in the top 3 out of 156 every year (Sadeghi, 2021).

This was just part of the research that piqued my interest in the Danish way of parenting, and what I learned gave me the method I was seeking to raise my children the way I wanted. I appreciated that the Danish school system supports playtime so much that it is built into the way they learn. I was also intrigued by their family life; Danish parenting perfectly blends democracy and authority to give children the freedom to be independent while still providing ground rules. They give their children a roadmap to follow, which encourages them to express themselves without crossing boundaries.

In my research, I've found that Danish families are good at open communication and understanding. The culture realizes how important it is for children to have even a little control over their lives. As parents, it's easy to take away that control, but it's not something we do consciously. Instead, it's something we do unconsciously as it's normal for us to think we know best. Unfortunately, this means we don't give our kids the courtesy of trying to understand what they want, and most of the time we don't encourage them to use their voice to let us know what that is. But the Danish parenting style feels like one that always listens and tries to understand, thereby creating a home in which everyone feels heard.

Parenting Style

Part of my research focused on learning the different parenting styles and identifying which one Danish families practice. There are four main parenting styles that I will mention. While I'll list them each here, going into a detailed discussion of each one is beyond the scope of this book; however, if you're intrigued, there are many resources available that focus specifically on these four styles. They are

- authoritarian parenting

- authoritative parenting

- permissive parenting

- uninvolved parenting

Danish families follow the authoritative parenting style, which is also the one I would have chosen if I simply picked between these four styles after researching them. To begin with, according to a report published by the National Library of Medicine, the authoritative style is the healthiest for kids (Sanvictores & Mendez, 2022). It requires patience and effort from both children and parents; while this can be a big commitment, it's worth it.

The authoritative parenting style is very democratic, and authoritative parents have high expectations. However, within those parameters, parents can also be quite flexible. They are willing to adjust their approach to adapt to each new situation.

What Democracy Looks Like in a Family

In the Danish households, everyone is a member of a mini-democracy. The children are not simply told what to do; they are allowed to be part of the decision-making process. Allowing children to play a role in making decisions gives them a sense of value while allowing them to work on their communication skills. We all know that a vital part of arguing your case in any decision-making process is the ability to communicate effectively.

Now, many parents and grandparents might argue that by allowing kids to make their own decisions, we're giving them too much power. However, within the Danish community, parents let their children give input into decisions in a way that includes a safety net of rules and consistency. This keeps the children on track while allowing them to take control of their own lives by having a say in what happens to and for them. By keeping rules in place while decisions are being made, parents ensure that their children make safe and reasonable choices.

That means within Danish families, the children have input on creating responsible rules and setting up the related consequences. Problem-solving is a family affair. When a family problem comes up, the entire family talks about the following:

- **Desired outcome:** When a problem has come up, either between the whole family or just the siblings, the kids and the parents discuss what they want to see happen. What is the outcome that they can all agree upon? Their focus is to establish the desired outcome and then work backward from there. Once the family agrees on what they want to see happen, they can then determine each person's part in the conflict and how to resolve it.

- **Needed boundaries or rules:** The family works together to determine if any rules need to be made to prevent the problem from occurring again. However, both the parents and the children are encouraged to share any boundaries they need regarding the conflict to feel safe and heard in future conversations.

- **Agreed-upon consequences:** The whole family agrees on the consequences of the actions. The kids are not just allowed but expected to give their opinions. They think through the problem and then determine what the consequence should be.

When my husband and I began using this parenting style, we guided the kids to see the difference between natural and related consequences. After a while, they learned to quickly realize which outcome their decisions would bring about.

The Importance of Problem-Solving as a Family

These family problem-solving sessions are not times when the parents get to unilaterally decide what needs to be done. They are not lecturing the children about what happened; they are simply trying to work through a problem in the most responsible, democratic way possible. They take all opinions and feelings into account while trying to come up with the best solution.

One of the biggest tools that comes from working through problems together is that our children learn how to problem-solve. They understand the importance of hearing the thoughts and opinions of others to reach an outcome that everyone agrees with and will adhere to.

What is important to remember is that once the rules and consequences have been set, the whole family abides by them. The parents don't change them midway through because they're frustrated or angry. The children don't get to change their minds because they are on the receiving end of the consequences. The reasons behind the consequences have been thoroughly discussed, the whole family has talked about how the problem made each of them feel, and they've made the best decision for their entire family.

We have experienced this in our own family. We homeschool the children, but there is a large age gap between the kids that started to cause a particular problem. My husband and I finally decided the problem needed to be addressed in a family council where we could approach the problem and find a solution together. I let the kids know that I was seeing them constantly interrupt each other during the learning portion of our day. I asked for ideas from each of them as to what they thought the ideal learning environment should look like. We went over how everyone felt when they were being interrupted and how they felt when the session went smoothly. After we heard everyone out, we discussed solutions and consequences. The outcome was that the kids agreed if one interrupted the other, they would have to go outside and take a walk around our cul-de-sac. We liked this consequence as it helped reset the behavior and separated the two. We often keep this in mind and have taught the kids to think how the consequence is to be one that is related to the situation. They all had to take that walk a couple of times, but I often tried to redirect their interruptions and reminded them of the consequences if they continued their disruptive behavior. It worked out well for the family because we made the rules and set up the consequences together, as a team.

Family Expectations

As a child, I remember how frustrating it was to realize the expectations my parents had for me without creating a solid family support system to help me meet them. The Danish style of parenting is effective and helpful because even though it's characterized by high demands and responsiveness, the demands are reasonable. Danish parents make sure the expectations for their children are realistic because they give them the resources and support needed.

There are some specific characteristics of the Danish parenting style that I'd like to note. First, children are allowed, and indeed encouraged, to express opinions and discuss options. Second, parents support their children as independent thinkers with the ability to reason through decisions. Third, a broken family rule earns fair and consistent discipline rather than harsh punishment. Finally, while parents place limits, expectations, and consequences on children's behavior, they also listen to their children and respond with warmth and nurturing.

It's been my experience that many people have strong opinions about this type of parenting, especially when they hear that children are allowed to voice their opinions and have a say in what goes on within the household. They automatically assume that children are never disciplined and they are allowed free rein to do whatever they want.

This couldn't be farther from the truth. Yes, Danish parents give their children the freedom to express their opinions and have a say in what happens to them, but the children also recognize there are rules, and those rules are there for a reason. The children also understand there are consequences for breaking the rules, and the whole family has come to a mutual decision about what those consequences will be. The consequences might be a little different than what you're used to since they aren't harsh, unforgiving or overly permissive, but they are effective.

Discipline styles vary wildly within families, but here is an example of how their parenting supports the discipline process. When a child does wrong, the parents hand out the agreed-upon punishment that the family puts together as a team. This is so important, especially since we've seen why it's key for discipline to be fair and consistent. In these families, not only do parents hand out the necessary discipline, but they also talk to their children. They have a conversation to get to the heart of the matter instead of yelling and throwing around random accusations or harsh words. The parents get to the core of the matter and try to find out why their child did whatever earned the consequences. Then they have a conversation to explain why that action was wrong. Parents talk through with the child what they could have done differently. We would all want our children to think before they act: to consider the natural consequences, and the discipline, behind their actions.

The benefit of raising your child with the Danish method is that you are giving them support and guidance while still showing love. Yes, children need to be disciplined when they do wrong. However, they don't need to be severely punished, and most importantly they must understand what they did wrong. Teach your child why wrongdoing is wrong instead of saying "Don't do it again" or using extreme discipline. Children can reason, so give them the tools they need to reason through an issue in order to learn from it.

My husband and I both valued allowing our kids to learn from their mistakes while they were young. Naturally, we all make mistakes— even as adults—but some of the life lessons that kids need to learn are better taught while they're young and the consequences are less drastic. As we get bigger, our errors get bigger, so let's teach our kids how to handle their own mishaps when they're still just little problems.

Studies show that children raised in the Danish parenting style are more likely to be capable, happy, and successful (Sanvictores & Mendez, 2022). This happens because, by raising children with these parenting techniques, you will also teach them abilities that will carry them through a wide variety of situations in life, including into adulthood. For instance, they'll develop self-confidence, which leads to emotional awareness and the ability to regulate their emotions. They will, in general, have happy dispositions, and all of these things increase a child's social skills.

Not only are children happier when they are raised this way, but they have better relationships, an increased ability to problem-solve, more creativity, better self-esteem, the ability to rely on themselves if needed, and overall satisfaction with their life—something that is vital for teens and young adults (Cherry, 2023b). The world throws a lot at us, but my experience using Danish parenting techniques within my family has taught me that children should learn the tools they need to survive at home with the loving support of their parents. We can't just give our kids the ability to cook, clean, and pay their bills; we need to teach them how to navigate the ups and downs of life.

Remember, though, that it might be a bit of a challenge to adapt to this parenting style. We only know what we were taught, and not everyone was raised in the Danish manner, so once we're parents, it doesn't matter how we *want* to raise children—there may be a stiff learning curve. There are some important things to keep in mind when you start down this road:

1. You will be a role model for your child; therefore, you must show them the same behaviors you expect from them. Remember, kids watch everything we do and they will imitate your behavior.

2. Be consistent with rules and discipline as we talked about above.

3. Exhibit good emotional understanding and control. This is another example where the children imitate their parents, and if you show them how, they will learn how to manage their emotions. This will also help with empathy so they can better understand others.

4. Children need to learn to act independently. Yes, there are still rules to follow and we must still expect them to do certain things. However, children must learn self-esteem and self-confidence, and this is accomplished through getting things done on their own.

5. Remain mindful of your actions while you're learning how to develop this parenting style. It might be a good idea to stay open with your children, as well, since children need to know their parents are human. This does not mean you should expose all your weaknesses to them because we are still superheroes to our kids. But they do need to know that mistakes are made by all and it's what you learn from your mistakes that is most important.

Responsibilities and Independence

Now that you understand the framework for the Danish parenting style, let's get into some specifics. First, it's important to recognize that these families begin their parenting journey with a very significant frame of mind. It is common for adults and parents to view children, including their own, as little humans with the capacity for wrongdoing. We've all heard parents talk about what little terrors their kids are, the "terrible twos," or how their kids are just waiting to get into mischief when unsupervised.

Danish families, though, have a different take on children. They see children as intrinsically good, and their parenting style reflects that. Rather than assume that children will get into trouble because they're naughty, they recognize that everyone wanders off the path sometimes but can learn from their mistakes. These parents fully embrace the concept that if we, as adults, can't be perfect, why would we expect perfection from our children?

I have tried to adopt that mindset, especially with my daughter, when I am at a park or group activity and she is lashing out at me while I am talking to another adult. It helps to take a minute to remember, she is a human being with needs, who is trying to convey something to me the best she can, with whatever is happening below the surface, and it's not that she is naughty. When I go through my check list of what might be the core of her frustration or behavior, which for her would be hungry, tired or too hot, or hurt feelings, but each child is a little different, I am able to show her empathy. This allows me to better help her as well as see her as inherently good. Having more of these interactions creates a more positive feeling towards my daughter and having that perspective creates a better feeling between us. It also makes a difference in the way I behave, talk to her and the way I talk about her.

Danish parents understand the value of teaching their children responsibilities. They recognize when they help their children set up a system to remember to feed the dog every day, for example, they are helping their children learn how to manage themselves. Parents work toward the goal of making sure their children can survive on their own in adulthood. What better way to do that than by teaching responsibility while they're young?

Within Danish households, children help out by keeping the home tidy. Every family member has chores to perform daily so that the entire workload does not fall on one family member. Routine tasks, like washing dishes, laundry, or sweeping, are not just considered chores. They are opportunities for teamwork and growth, and kids have a front-row seat. Making a bed or setting the table is not just a chore, it's instilling a sense of responsibility and independence in the child from an early age. More then not these parents don't have to wait until bedtime to clean up their child's toys. Instead, the child proudly puts their toys away when they're done playing with them (of course, this is accomplished once we have laid the groundwork with our kids.)

Children develop a strong sense of ownership and capability by participating in household tasks. They learn how to contribute and be a part of something bigger while learning the valuable life skills they will need for adulthood.

Balancing Work and Family Life

Within Danish families, it is understood that family comes first. Work should never overshadow the quality time a family spends together. I am going to lay out the details that make it possible for Danish parents to place family above work. Then I will outline how this can be done within other societies or cultures, since not all countries have the same workplace and governmental policies that Denmark offers. Danish culture has made balancing work and family more than just a concept. It is a way of life.

Denmark seems to have a handle on work/life balance, and it shows in the policies they've put in place for workers. The Organization for Economic Cooperation and Development (OECD) has performed extensive research on workplace policies within various countries. As a global institution, its purpose is to build working policies that will "stimulate economic progress and world trade" (Bardoloi, 2018). This is accomplished by understanding the working policies within its member countries; I'll rely heavily on OECD research in the next section.

Extensive Parental Leave Policies

Danish companies give their employees an extensive parental leave plan. In 2022, the Denmark parental leave system was reformed. Parents receive a total of 52 weeks of leave, with mothers entitled to 4 weeks before the arrival of their child. After the child's birth, the mother can take an additional 14 weeks. The father can take 2 weeks during this time, as well. After this, the parents can share an additional 32 weeks of leave. This leave can be shared or transferred between parents (*Maternity Leave and Paternity Leave When Working in Denmark*, 2024).

Parents can extend their leave for up to 14 weeks in certain circumstances. The financial support during the parental leave period is commendable also, as parents are paid the entire time. If you want to explore the regulations surrounding parental leave in more depth, go to www.lifeindenmark.dk. The website gives information about qualifications for government assistance and the corresponding payment amount.

Companies in Denmark strive to give their employees plenty of flexibility for things like family medical and dental appointments. All these workplace regulations help employees stay happier at work and home.

Flexible Work Hours

In Denmark, the work week is officially 37 hours, and extra hours are discouraged. Employees generally don't work past 4:00 p.m., giving them time to pick kids up from school and start the evening meal (Russell, 2016). We know that being overworked can lead to stress that manifests in many ways, including a lack of patience with our loved ones. It is so much easier to implement the Danish parenting style when a parent's stress level is manageable.

State-Subsidized Daycare

Women have better opportunities to work outside the home in Denmark due to the supportive network that provides daycare for working parents. In many countries, families struggle because daycare is either difficult to find or is so expensive that it is almost not worth having both parents work outside the home. Danish culture has removed that stress within families, allowing parents to work while utilizing onsite daycare facilities.

Paid Holidays

In Denmark, employees are entitled to five weeks, stipulated by the Holiday Act, of paid holiday per year, which is equivalent to 2.08 days for each month worked. Those that are employed full time by the state or municipality (public sector) get other holiday entitlements (Feriefridage) which are paid holidays in addition to those five weeks. Research has been conducted on productivity and its relationship with hours worked. (Luxton, 2016) Which has revealed that productivity decreases as more hours worked increases. Danish society understands this in a way that they take holidays to relax, be with family and rejuvenate, as well as taking breaks in the day, to be with other coworkers or time to reset. The Danish philosophies of lagom and hygge, discussed later in the book, give the society a sense of contentment and are a part of why they are suggested to be the happiest people in the world. In my estimation, hygge is the biggest reason Danish people are given that title "the happiest people in the world" and have family lives that work so well. In the next chapter I discuss how hygge creates the cozy, contented feelings that the Danish people surround themselves with every day.

The Balance of Work and Family Outside of Denmark

In most other cultures, work life overshadows family life, with many parents working over 40 hours each week, coming home late, and relying on takeout for dinners. I think many ask and wonder how it will be possible to create a balance of work and family life. We once had some dear friends who had a small, family-run business. Unfortunately, they worked seven days a week with no vacations. Yes, their kids have an excellent work ethic since they saw their parents do nothing but work, but the parents now wonder if it was worth it. They feel like they missed out on more than they should have with their children, and their memories of work aren't as precious as those moments with their children.

Not every country has the same workplace practices that allow parents to navigate the balance between family and work successfully.

So, how do we go about balancing our work and family life if we don't live in Denmark, with its policies that promote this balance? Most often, both parents must work to pay the bills, so the idea that one parent gets to stay home or even work from home is not always possible.

Therefore, balancing work and family life is a daily, conscious decision. But the biggest aspect of the decision is to leave work where it belongs—at work. When you are home, be present for your family. Head outside with your family; it doesn't have to be a big production. Take a simple walk, visit the park, or do a quick hike on some trails near your neighborhood. Even playing in the backyard is a wonderful way to spend time together.

Building the feeling of contentment that comes with hygge is the goal, even if all you can do is spend half a day on the weekend with your family. When it snows, build a snowman with the kids. After work, spend time with the family at the dinner table talking about the day. Institute a family game night once a week or even once a month if that's all you have time for.

The bottom line is that you try to make the most of your family time. Whether it's unplanned or planned, family time builds memories and creates an unshakeable bond between you and your children. My husband and I discovered the traditions we put in place with our children made much more of an impact on them than just about anything else.

When we are struggling, be it overworked or mistakes made, we find it is the traditions we have created, like family game time, attending church, prayer or taking walks to talk or imagine together, that resets our family. When we keep to those healthy, positive traditions, even though we might find we don't have time or desire, due to our stress, it reminds us what matters most in those difficult times. My husband left his time consuming corporate job to allow us to travel and live out of the country for a while. We lost both of our fathers years before, so we wanted to have life experiences with our kids before they grew up or if something happened to change within our family. Our goal was also to world school our kids as well as have time to focus on our family relationships and improve our businesses. It was a leap of faith and difficult for our family to move from one place to another as we were housesitting for our lodging. However, we saw that the foundation we built allowed for open communication when things were rough. It also helped the kids to know what they could expect in the week, with the preset traditions that created a sense of unity and joy in our family.

Navigating Gender Equality

It would be great to say that Danish families have smashed the inequality between genders in the office and the home. While this is not the case, Denmark scores an impressive 77.5 out of 100 in gender equality rankings (Risman, 2020). Gender equality has a vital part to play within the Danish parenting style, so even though the country is not at 100%, they are doing their part and it is worth mentioning.

Within the Danish parenting style, everyone has a part to play. Gender is not a barrier, but it also doesn't give anyone an extra vote or a bigger part to play. Mothers and fathers work together and respect each other as equals.

Men and women are champions of each other's rights and chores within the household, but these are not designated based on traditional, constrained roles. The parents use this concept as the perfect way to lead by example. In some cultures, it is common to find the patriarch of the family spending time performing household repairs or completing a "honey-do" list, while the matriarch cooks the meals, tends to the kids, and generally manages the kitchen.

However, parenting this way limits children and their skills. It's better to teach them all chores are equal, and that the father can cook dinner and do dishes if the mom is busy repairing the refrigerator. In fact, this means when our children are grown, they can take care of themselves as needed.

Traveling Cultural Paths

No matter how much we like the Danish parenting style, some potential challenges and drawbacks may arise when we try to apply their approach within diverse cultural contexts. As we all understand, cultural differences lead to differences in parenting, so often trying to incorporate the Danish style into another culture can be like fitting a square peg into a round hole. For example, maybe your culture values a more hierarchical parent-child relationship. The open communication that the Danish family enjoys will not be an easy transition for all your family members.

Danish parenting facilitates independence, while many cultures emphasize following directions, doing what you're told, and so on. Finding your way through these differences can be like navigating a maze; we need to learn how to find that perfect spot between embracing new ideas while still honoring our cultural roots.

One of the biggest obstacles I faced when implementing the Danish parenting style into my family was their philosophy about children and self-expression. I came from a family that placed a high value on traditional obedience, and many of the decisions I made regarding my children caused dissent, especially among my grandparents. In Denmark, every generation follows these parenting practices, so it is not a part of the child-rearing process that raises eyebrows. In my family's culture, however, I heard some scathing opinions from other adults and grandparents about what they considered as ruining my children.

Parents need to keep in mind that it is vital to practice cultural sensitivity when implementing the Danish parenting style into their household. It took me a while to realize that it wasn't going to do any good to completely alienate my extended family. I needed to learn how to meld the Danish culture with my own, but it took time. I just had to figure out how to take parts of Danish parenting and adapt them to my way of life. There is no specific guidebook for this—any more than there is for parenting—as it's a road each parent has to navigate on their own.

There's good news, though! Some parts of Danish parenting translate to other cultures easily. For example, the empathy that I began working on with my children easily transferred to how my own culture valued respect. It turned out that my grandparents' biggest concern was that they felt I wasn't teaching my children to respect their elders.

My grandfather's fear arose when one of my children's behaviors was not in alignment with his beliefs that when an adult speaks, the children are expected to do as they are told without question. He especially took offense and decided that I was raising my children without respect for parents or other adults. However after some time with my children, he changed his opinion when he witnessed the empathy that had developed strongly in both of my kids. He viewed my kid's empathy as respect and it eased his mind. In fact, my children's empathy helped them recognize their grandparents' different cultural lifestyles. Because it was a topic their father and I discussed with them, they understood when to ease up on their own opinions and behavior. Eventually, my grandfather even started asking for their opinions, and a blend of cultures was born.

We all have to navigate the twists and turns of life's journey, and parenting is no different. Detours arise, and we need to determine the new path to reach our destination without too many bumps and potholes or getting lost along the way. The cultural differences we must face represent bumpy roads, but we can learn how to tailor Danish parenting to fit our own cultures.

One of the intriguing concepts I encountered in Danish culture is *Janteloven* (yanteh-loven), also known as the Law of Jante. Originating as a satirical concept in Danish literature, Janteloven is traditionally seen as a critical lens on a societal tendency to prioritize community over individuality, often discouraging self-promotion and standing out. While not explicitly applied in Danish parenting, it subtly influences how many Danes think about humility, collective well-being, and maintaining balance in social relationships.

Janteloven might be interpreted as advocating for a spirit of cooperation and community harmony, yet it is generally understood as a caution against ego and an encouragement to contribute meaningfully without needing recognition. In parenting, Danes focus more directly on values like empathy, cooperation, and community responsibility, fostering these traits in their children through daily interactions and family life rather than explicit adherence to Janteloven itself.

In reflecting on Danish culture, I realized I could encourage my children to develop empathy and kindness, contributing positively to the family and community, without feeling the need to diminish their uniqueness. In our family, individuality is balanced with respect and compassion for others, teaching our children they can express their personalities and talents while being mindful of the team spirit that Danish families value so deeply.

This blending of values creates a supportive environment where children can grow both independently and within a close-knit family, preparing them for the broader world where kindness and community are strengths. We found that taking inspiration from Danish values allowed us to foster a sense of belonging and resilience without losing the vibrant individuality that makes our family unique.

Picking and choosing certain parts of Danish parenting techniques doesn't mean you aren't utilizing their excellent methods to the fullest; it just means you're using what will fit your family. Remember, I mentioned that our rules were tailored to fit our family, and that is something that can be said for anyone's household. We are all different; we come from many backgrounds, and it's vital to recognize that we should keep what makes us different because it's what makes us special. But we can mix it up a bit and try something new that resonates with how we want to live.

More Resources to Explore

My parenting journey has been priceless and my memories with my children have been precious. My husband and I actively changed our parenting because we knew there was something mentally and emotionally healthier than what we remembered as children, and we wanted our kids to have that experience.

In the journey to find the right parenting style for our family, I also discovered other resources that can be integrated right into the Danish style of parenting. These philosophies and activities share many concepts and desired outcomes.

The first resource I discovered was in my youth when working with my best friend's mother at her daycare. She had us attend training on the Love and Logic philosophy as outlined in this book *Parenting with Love and Logic* by Foster Cline and Jim Fay. In brief the book explains that parents are to provide an atmosphere of love, acceptance, and empathy while allowing the natural consequences of a child's behavior and actions to do the teaching. This aligns perfectly with the Danish parenting style.

We also, as a family, took the Enneagram Personality Test (Quiz, n.d.). Remember, I mentioned in the Introduction that everyone has their own personality, which influences how they learn and how they respond to problems. My husband and I felt that if we understood everyone's personalities better, we would be more equipped to deal with any problem that might arise.

Along with this personality test, I have been reading the book *The Child Whisperer* by Carol Tuttle (2012). This book has really opened my eyes to the four different types of children and where my own children fall. The four types include

Fun-loving: Type 1

Sensitive: Type 2

Determined: Type 3

Serious: Type 4

Knowing these types has helped me learn how each of my kids needs something different from me. It has taught me how each one will react, along with what they can and cannot handle. In turn, I have learned how to show them love and appreciation because it has opened my eyes to realizing we don't all receive care or love in the same way (Tuttle, 2012).

As I've mentioned, though, the beauty of Danish parenting is that we can take what works for our family and augment it with other different ideas. Most of the ideas that I have discovered through my research fit into the Danish parenting style like puzzle pieces. For instance, the Conscious Discipline method is one we have embraced within our family.

The Conscious Discipline method showed my husband and me how to help our children through their more difficult moments (*Conscious Discipline Methodology*, n.d.). Children must learn how to manage their anger, how to effectively stop bullying, how to control their impulses, and how to learn from their mistakes. Thanks to the Conscious Discipline method, we learned the seven skills necessary to help our children through these processes:

- composure

- encouragement

- assertiveness

- choices

- empathy

- positive intent

- consequences

I encourage you to visit the website consciousdiscipline.com/methodology/ and learn more about this philosophy, which many teachers and parents are implementing in their classrooms and homes.

Of course, I recognized right away that the only way I was going to parent successfully was to recognize that I was part of the problem when it came to my kids. So my husband and I had to find something that would help us work on ourselves. We discovered the Arbinger Institute and its Leadership and Self-Deception portion. The last part of that is misleading, I know, but self-deception simply means that we don't know we have a problem. When we aren't aware of the role we are playing, we become the primary source of conflict (*Leadership and Self-Deception Overview*, n.d.). So we spent time working to become the best versions of ourselves to help our kids become their own best selves.

The Danish parenting style is simply a piece of the parenting journey our family has been traveling. Listed below are components that we've taken from these other resources and added to our parenting journey.

Disagree Appropriately

My family has spent a lot of time learning how to openly communicate and create an environment that makes the kids feel safe. They know that they can disagree with us, but we have also ensured that they understand how to "appropriately" disagree with us. This has been a huge asset in our family life, since it allows our children the ability to express their opinions—a skill we know they're going to need out in the real world. Our children learn how to disagree without being rude or disrespectful, and it's better to learn this skill now while they're young. They have to understand the reasons behind their disagreement without doing it just because they can, and this gives us the chance to understand or recognize when we're being repressive or controlling. For example our children will tell us what they heard us say to them, share with us how they feel about it and what they may want to do instead or change about what we asked. We then have opened communication to hear them out and say yes if it's in the parameters of family values and plans. This has been a huge game-changer for our family, building trust, respect, and understanding while also teaching us patience, kindness, and empathy.

Read and Tell Stories Together

When my children were younger we read a lot of children's books together, and we still tell stories about how to understand other kids and their feelings. This boosts our children's empathy, but it also helps my husband and I understand how to "read" our kids. Just because we're the parents doesn't mean we can read their minds. Since they have their own unique personalities, sometimes we need a lot of clues to understand what's going through their minds and hearts. We don't just read; we talk about the stories. Quality children's books especially can bring up questions for a child, and we encourage them to ask those questions.

We want them to ask "Why?" and more importantly, even harder questions—the ones that parents usually shy away from because they don't know how to answer. Since we are, in a sense, telling our children we've got their backs, we need to prove it. Therefore, when difficult questions come up, we don't sweep them under the rug or defer to the other parent on a later day. We talk it out, and my husband and I are very good at being honest with the kids when we're not sure what to say or how to say it. We tell them why we don't know and we have the most truthful conversation possible.

What we've also learned, though, is that it's important to stay on track. Naturally, we try to keep our answers age-appropriate, but sometimes parents can wander off-topic. We end up giving too much information or answering a question the child wasn't asking. What my husband and I have learned is to ask if they have more questions or something else they want to talk about, and we always thank them for asking and coming to us for the answers.

Become Your Child's Self-Talk

My husband and I try not to let the kids go to sleep without letting them know how much we appreciate them and how much we love them. We like to take a few moments with each child before bed, telling them about one thing that stood out during the day we enjoyed or that was empathetic of them. We want our kids to remember these moments so that when they get older and become adults, our words of encouragement and love become their own self-talk. Rather than absorbing what is negative out in the world, we want them to breathe in all our love and compassion and then take it into themselves as their own.

Reviewing the Highlights of the Danish Parenting Style

Have you decided the road you want to take on your parenting journey? Here is a checklist to help you map out your route, and understand whether Danish parenting will fit your family.

- **Empowering independence:** Is it your goal to nurture self-sufficiency in your children? The Danish parenting style encourages kids to take on responsibilities that help them become self-sufficient adults.

- **Respecting autonomy:** Does your vision for your family include open communication? Danish parenting considers it vital that children have a voice and family decisions are a team effort.

- **Structured freedom:** Is it your ultimate goal to provide a secure framework while also allowing your children to choose and express their own thoughts and emotions? Danish parenting sets rules while also respecting feelings and remaining flexible to adapt to circumstance.

- **Cultural harmony:** Can you incorporate the Danish parenting style into your cultural context? Danish parenting allows you to gather the best tools for your cultural values and helps you mesh them into your family life.

If you have answered yes to these you are in the right place! This book will expand and share on these main topics and more. Keep going on this quest for knowledge, and congratulations on being a mother or father, it is the most important and rewarding journey of your life.

Let's Talk About Hygge

The Art of Cozy Contentment

In the previous chapter we talked about how part of Danish parenting is a product of hygge, but let's go a little further in this chapter to explore hygge in depth.

Hygge is not just a Danish concept; it is the backbone of Nordic culture. In 2023, the Gallup World Happiness Report listed Denmark as second in ranking between Finland (first) and Iceland (third) (World Happiness Report, 2023). The report focuses on different aspects of a country's social environment. In Denmark, the social environment is shaped by having reliable support systems, the freedom to make life choices, and a strong sense of trust and generosity.

Denmark has been first on the Happiness Report several times, but often the country falls somewhere in the top 10, along with other Nordic countries who prioritize hygge. According to the Gallup report, citizens in Denmark are hugely satisfied with their lives. They have reliable welfare benefits, corruption is low, democracy and state institutions are effective and in a good state of repair, and the country has a small population (Altman, 2016).

Denmark is also one of the least corrupt countries in the world because of commitment to freedom of the press. They give almost unlimited access to information, and their judicial systems are independent with their public officials holding strong standards of integrity.

But the most important part of what brings the Danish people such happiness, or contentment, is a vital part of their social construct: hygge.

Hygge refers to high-quality social interactions and is a part of Danish culture in more than just family life. It can be used as a noun, adjective, or even a verb. But overall, not only does it translate to "cozy," but it refers to the intentional intimacy that takes place when you experience moments that are balanced, harmonious, and safe. This strengthens trust and builds camaraderie.

Danish families build a sense of hygge within their family units, which includes people who are visiting them. Unlike other countries where happiness is income-generated, the Danish people instead place their happiness within hygge, which greatly reduces their stress.

The Essence of Hygge and Well-Being

Hygge is associated with "relaxation, indulgence, and gratitude" and has been defined as "taking pleasure in the presence of gentle, soothing things" (Altman, 2016). This concept of Scandinavian coziness has become an international sensation. The Danish people use hygge to create an oasis in the middle of the very real, very hectic world that we live in. It's a way to escape unrest. I always associate hygge with the atmosphere that is created within the Danish family. I find hygge to be cozy, in the moments when I'm most content. Most importantly, hygge comes to me when I take the time to focus on the little things, like how I feel when I'm curled up by the fire with my family or how an afternoon spent reading a book with a cup of hot cocoa makes me feel.

According to Merriam-Webster, the simplest definition of "essence" is the basic nature of a thing; the quality or qualities that make a thing what it is (Merriam-Webster, n.d.-a). Hygge is an essence—it is the simple, cozy, comfortable feeling of life found when you embrace the simple things like a walk in nature, game night with the family, or time spent sharing special moments with loved ones.

Most of us are looking for contentment in our lives. We crave a happy, stable home where we can find real contentment and those cozy feelings we imagine when we look at our favorite paintings. You know—the ones that bring joy when you look at them, the ones that "speak" to you somehow. A friend of mine has a painting that she says gives her comfort. When she looks at it, she has an immediate sense of calm. This is what I'm talking about. But hygge is more than what is tangible; it is the environment where positive emotions flourish. Think of hygge as the compass that guides us toward a rich, inner peace, and fulfilling life.

Truly understanding the concept of hygge as well as the Danish parenting style will create this way of life and feeling we're looking for. It is possible to recreate this feeling in our homes and in our lives. Maybe our sense of hygge won't look exactly like it does in Denmark, because it will be what we've tailored to fit our family and lifestyle. Danish families incorporate hygge through interior design and food, which is something we can easily work into our own lives. The seasons can bring in a sense of hygge, as well, which is something that appealed to me.

I have always associated the concept of hygge with the way my world feels during the holidays. Family, music and food take center stage during the holiday season, and the warmth I get from those things makes the holidays my favorite time of year. The love I feel from family, friends and the contentment from good times made everything feel cozy and comforting.

What my husband and I discovered was that we didn't want hygge to be there only during the holidays. One thing we have done, that continues today, is our special dessert and movie time as a family. Sometimes life would get hectic during the week but we could all look forward to our family movie night with a special treat. We also love to be with other people and have made it a priority to spend time with those around us. Whether it be together visiting over food or a game, the time spent with one another made a huge difference in keeping that feeling last all year long. Inviting others into our home throughout the year for food, games, and good company has brought a special sense of joy. We understood that there were going to be pitfalls and that not every day was going to be exactly what we wanted, but we were willing to try. At the end of the day, we determined that the hours we worked or even how much money we made wasn't important. We wanted to be realistic and understand that our income helped with the overall feeling of contentment, but what would last forever was the time spent with our children and the memories we created as a family.

Examples of Hygge

To some cultures, hygge can come across as smug, especially since it is often mentioned in the same sentence when people talk about Danish people being the happiest people in the world. But it's easier to appreciate the concept of hygge when you put everything in perspective and realize more money isn't what makes you happy. It's the little things, the stuff you have and do regardless of the amount of money you have. Money can't touch the sense of happiness and togetherness a family gets from spending time together, creating memories to last a lifetime.

Within our own family, we put together some family events to nurture that feeling of hygge. For a season every Monday night we all cooked dinner together. The menu was determined the previous week, and the meal was chosen by a different family member each time. We ate together with no cell phones and just talked about our day. At first, the kids weren't sure if they liked it but soon it became their favorite day of the week. Our time sitting around the table got longer and longer after the meal was over as we laughed, talked, and shared stories. My kids love to share their dreams during breakfast time if they had any that night. The kids didn't want to give up the camaraderie and happy feelings we all had from spending quality time together. They will ask to cook together and we find cooking breakfast lately has given these same kinds of feelings. We are glad we took the time and effort into creating these cherished traditions to keep us grounded.

One of my other favorite traditions has been our family walks, where we explored new places together. During the walk my husband often started telling stories; sometimes we made up games to play along the way, or we sang together. I loved these times because we felt so close doing something so simple but with such an impact on our lives.

We had a once-a-week game night as well. These nights turned into more laughing than playing sometimes, and it didn't matter what the game was that night—we all enjoyed it. What we discovered as a family was that we didn't need to do things together every moment of every day, but we did need to grab onto the times we had together and make the most of them. It took a little bit of effort to rearrange our patterns, but once we did, we discovered that we were building the kind of memories with our kids that would last a lifetime.

Statistics and Facts We Need to Understand Hygge

How does Danish culture achieve the level of contentment with life in general that allows them to embrace family life in their way? We've read how happy they are and how they take that happiness and create a comfortable, all-inclusive, warm family life. We all want to do that. But what external factors are needed to accomplish this goal? Let's talk about it.

To start, Denmark has some of the most efficient workers, primarily because the country's workplace standards allow them to maintain a healthy balance between home and work. Employers respect how important this balance is to their employees, and they take steps to ensure that everyone can "successfully combine work, family commitments and personal life" that is so "important for the well-being of all members of a household" (*Work-Life Balance*, 2014).

Drawbacks to More Hours Worked

Denmark's approach to balanced work and family life is a large part of what contributes to the country's sense of hygge. By keeping a balance between work and family, Danish people are able to create the sense of peace, coziness, and contentment that comes with hygge. Therefore, I want to briefly explain the consequences that come with an unbalanced home and work life.

Besides time not spent with family, there are drawbacks to working excessive hours. Although I've separated out each one and tried to be more specific about the particular side effect of overworking yourself, they are all related. Each one is a direct link to the other.

Health

Overworking yourself can be debilitating. Working excess hours by going in very early, coming home late, or both can cause the body to become run-down. Once this happens, it's difficult to avoid colds and flus, which run the body down even more. Consistently being sick is an indicator that your immune system is low and unable to fight off even the most basic germs.

Stress

When you work excess hours, it's easy to become stressed. It feels as though the work is never done, which piles on more stress since you go home feeling as though you haven't accomplished all that you should. Stress can add to poor health and can ultimately lead to more severe health concerns.

Overall Well-Being

Our overall well-being consists of our mental as well as physical health. It is so important to stay healthy, physically but also mentally. When you're stressed because of work, your mental well-being suffers in addition to your physical health. This leads to a decrease in overall health, since so often a decline in one aspect of health can lead to another.

Experiencing Hygge at Home

I have discovered that I can create the feeling of hygge when I'm home, even when I'm by myself. I have a little seat swing in a corner of a room where I go when I need to relax and recharge. I have a special quilt that I sit with when I'm in that chair, and my family knows it's my special place where I spend alone time; they respect that and leave me be while I'm there. It is a lovely spot and the sense of hygge and contentment I get while I'm relaxing in reading or journaling or listening to music is a time I also cherish for myself.

My daughter expressed a desire to have her own special place in her room, too. She wanted us to build her a little "tree" where she could create a nest, her own cozy spot she could snuggle into with her books and stuffies. My husband and I believe that we have successfully transmitted the concept of hygge to our kids.

Besides my seat swing, I get that sense of hygge from comfort food. When I feel stressed or overworked, most of the time it only takes a good plate of lasagna or veggies and rice with nori. Along with my favorite quilt, music and/or a good book to wipe out all that stress and tension. I feel like it's called relaxation and comfort food for a reason.

My brother and his wife have created a very special sense of hygge at home, as well. They have six children, and once a month they sit down with the whole family to read poetry and have tea and cookies. It's a special time for the whole family and they love the sense of hygge they get from the time together. It's so simple, but so special.

A friend of mine has teatime with her 7-year-old daughter at least once a month. They both love it, even though they aren't doing anything that many people would consider exciting. They just talk, but the daughter loves that her mom is focused specifically on her and showing an interest in the stuff that she likes. What makes it so special is that the mother is "present." She is letting her daughter know she's important, and they're building memories together.

Hygge for Beginners, Beginning to Understand the Importance

The real estate company John L. Scott recently put out a short article about creating hygge in the home, and I found it appealing and something I think most people would be able to easily accomplish (*Hygge,* n.d.). It's a bit of "hygge for beginners," since it's something we can all do even if we don't completely understand hygge yet. Here are the four tips they suggest to create hygge in your home:

1. **Brighten up your living space:** Over time, a home can start to feel dingy. Correcting this is a simple fix. Clean dirty light bulbs, allowing more light to project into the room. The biggest fix, though, is to wash your windows. The natural light comes through more brightly and can lighten the mood. Candles are also a home brightener; even better, their smell can bring to mind the feelings or memories you're looking for in your living space.

2. **Seal up leaks:** We all have those drafty areas in our house that create cold spots, which doesn't lend to the cozy feeling you're looking for with hygge. Search out those cold spots and seal them up. Keeping out the cold and keeping in the warm helps you create hygge.

3. **Switch from traditional wood or gas fireplaces:** the John L. Scott company recommends looking for a gel insert (*Hygge*, n.d.). It's eco-friendly, smoke-friendly, and puts out fewer allergens. The insert doesn't use gas, wood, or electricity to operate and if you get the right model, it even crackles like a real fire. Even better, there's no chimney to suck out the heat and let it escape from the house.

4. **Grow plants:** Many plants eat up the toxins that come from household cleaners. They also increase humidity levels, which cuts down on the dust in your home. Growing plants is rewarding, relaxing, and satisfying.

I think we've all felt hygge during our lives; we just didn't know it could be so important. Of course, if you're like me, you didn't know it was a philosophy and a way of life, and you certainly didn't realize it could be so easy to experience. I love this concept, especially within the context of my parenting journey. It has given my family so much joy, peace, and obvious contentment.

I've learned that hygge is something we can all create within our homes through practices as simple as relaxing with our family, telling stories, and laughing together. It sounds so simple, doesn't it? And it really is. I think we all reach a stage in life where we think we need "stuff" to be happy: the right furniture, the perfect house, our dream car—whatever possessions we grew up thinking we needed to reach success.

What is success, though? That is a question I have asked myself a lot, especially once I became a parent. I found that success was different than I imagined and I realized changing my perspective as well as my expectations added to this magic of parenting. It can be a real eye-opener when you realize that your ideas, opinions, and philosophies are going to be passed along to someone else. Suddenly you rethink everything you believe because you don't know if it's right and what you're sharing is going to do good or harm.

Having that sense of hygge in our home has been one of the most important steps in raising the capable, independent, empathetic children I knew my kids could be. There are still a lot of other lessons that come alongside hygge in parenting the Danish way and now it's time to get into those.

∞

Friluftsliv and Lagom

Danish and a Little bit of Swedish Philosophies

D anish parenting regularly incorporates certain activities that many other cultures view as a once-a-year event. For example, many families go camping, but only once or twice a year and only during the summer. But Danes believe that living close to nature should be a way of life for everyone. They don't limit time spent in nature to the warm days of summer; instead, they embrace the outdoors all year.

This love of outdoor time is called *friluftsliv*, "Free-Loofs-Leaf" and it's something Danish families use as part of hygge. Contrary to other cultures, the outdoor activities they enjoy are not simply for competition or sports. They want to spend time enjoying nature and all it has to offer. Because of this love of the outdoors, Danish children spend most of their time outside. It's no surprise that Denmark has a high percentage of eco-conscious citizens.

Friluftsliv, according to the author of the book *There's No Such Thing as Bad Weather*, is "loosely translated as open-air life" (McGurk, 2020, p. 12). It is this concept that has Danish children spending 20% of their school day outside at recess (McGurk, 2020). There are "forest schools," which are nurseries where the children spend the entire day outdoors learning from nature and the physical world around them. Danish people take outdoor life very seriously, and families extend that belief to their parenting styles.

It helps, of course, when the country has another concept called *allemansrätten, a more Swedish concept*. This is actually part of their constitution and is the right to freely roam. The only restriction is when the land is posted or private property. This gives children the opportunity to explore, have adventures, and learn the value of the ecosystem. As long as there is no harm done to the property, it is open for exploration.

What a wonderful concept, and one my husband and I fully embraced. We both grew up in a time where, if we weren't in school, our days were spent outdoors—riding bikes, creating forts in the desert ravine, climbing trees, and doing other kid stuff, but all outdoors. We went home with skinned knees, bruises, scrapes, and a few gravel burns from unwise bike-riding adventures, but we slept well and we felt good. The idea that fresh air is good for you is something we heard a lot when we were kids, and I imagine it's something Danish families say a lot, as well.

The few snow days we got when we were kids weren't spent indoors; instead, we headed outside, bundled up so tightly that only our eyes were showing and ready to tackle gravity with the thrilling possibility of taking flight as we careened our sleds down the steepest hill we could find. I have a friend who grew up in Alaska, and she remembers going to a camp—during the winter. All activities were outdoors, no matter how much snow was on the ground or how cold it was. That's how Danish families live with the *friluftsliv* concept.

According to Katie Arnold (2022), a journalist and editor for *Outdoor Online*, there are nine things we can do to incorporate *friluftsliv* into our lives no matter what our culture looks like.

She recommends that we start with the little things. Getting out in nature does not have to be a big production. It can be as simple as taking a walk in your neighborhood. The important thing is to let your kids explore. Don't hover over them. Remember, you're raising them to make smart choices and you've presumably given them the knowledge they need to avoid trouble and dangerous situations. Now trust them. Of course, take it in baby steps. Walk with your kids to the park and then maybe go to a nearby coffee shop while your kids play. It's not unreasonable to go over the rules with your children, whether that is meeting times or expectations and/or boundaries before you leave them at the park. It could be that you are just over on a bench watching them from a distance. You will be the one to know your area and kids best, so remember safety when leaving them alone. Finding places to let them experience nature and play as kids without adults supervising their every move will be of benefit for their growth.

Speaking of taking it slowly, if you're not ready to turn your kids loose at the neighborhood park without your supervision, think about turning your backyard into their playground. This can become a family project that the kids can take part in from start to finish. In fact, why not invite a few families in the neighborhood to join in both the building process and playtime? It doesn't have to be expensive. Go to a junkyard and look for wood scraps, metal pieces, or whatever you can find to build a playground. It doesn't have to be fancy, although you'll want to remove old nails and anything that might be harmful to a child. Kids will love the idea of building a bike ramp, a seesaw, or a fort.

Since we're on the subject of building your backyard mini-playground, this is a good time to bring up another of Arnold's ideas: allowing your children to take risks. I don't mean the kind of risks that come from playing in forts that still have rusty nails sticking out of the wood. I mean, once that playground is built, allowing your kids to take risks like using the bike ramp to climb trees, or creatively coming and going from a treehouse or fort. Let them figure out their boundaries and what they're comfortable with. These decision-making skills and finding out what they can do will be valuable assets when they're adults.

Now, Arnold specifically says that structured sports are not necessary for children, and she's correct. If your children want to play a sport, let them. But just playing outside is enough activity. If they want to play a sport, a game of basketball at the park or in your driveway is a good way for them to let off steam. I used to encourage my kids to get together with their friends and play a quick game of soccer at the park. A neighbor of ours put together what he called "Xtreme Frisbee golf" in his backyard. He had an overgrown, lumpy yard with small groves of trees and lots of overgrown grass. Every summer, he would host a neighborhood barbecue and the adults and children would play Xtreme frisbee golf in this overgrown jungle of a yard. The kids loved it.

If none of these ideas appeal to you, you don't have a safe park in your neighborhood, or the routes to your nearest park aren't safe, start a conversation with city officials. Don't take "No" for an answer. Have a plan in mind when you get their attention, and lay out ideas to make outdoor play fun and safe for neighborhood children. Then, keep it on their radar until they put a plan in motion. The bottom line is that if you want your kids to have the opportunity of safe play outside your yard, be their advocate. I have seen this in everything from small towns to the big cities, neighborhoods coming together to create play spaces for their kids. Sometimes it's wandering your area to find the small gems for places for your kids to explore, imagine and take those safe risks.

Of course, as Arnold says, it's sometimes up to the parents to get that outdoor play going. You have to promote *friluftsliv*, because most would rather stay inside and watch TV on a rainy or cloudy day. But as we've been told for generations, fresh air is good for us. So make it a habit for the whole family to get outdoors even when it's raining. If you've set a schedule for outdoor time and the rain starts, don't postpone it. Head out there and enjoy that fresh air. Before you head outside, though, remember that the other thing Arnold says is to dress for the weather. Always be prepared to spend time outside, but remember to make sure everyone participating is wearing the correct clothing for the adventure. Don't head out in the rain wearing sandals and a light sweater, for instance. Part of the healthy aspect of fresh air is being appropriately clothed when you're in it.

And last of all, Arnold wants parents to talk about outdoor time. Get other families to join you when you go to the park. Put together a committee to clean up the neighborhood park or sidewalks. I know that there can be unsafe areas within cities, and that leads to a natural fear of your children spending time outdoors. But there is research that shows "green spaces have a calming effect and can reduce violence" (Arnold, 2022). So don't think that just because you live in the city, none of these things can happen. Do your research and make yourself the squeaky wheel that gets things done.

Freedom and Responsibility: Self-Confidence

As I've mentioned, one of Danish parenting's desired outcomes is to give children the necessary tools to succeed in life as adults. I mentioned above that experiencing *friluftsliv* can build resilience, for one, and along with that comes self-confidence. As we know, better decision-making skills build self-confidence.

This mindset is vital to a successful adult life, since "adulting," as the kids call it, is difficult even at the best of times. Therefore, when we teach our children how to enjoy the freedom that comes with outdoor play while they're young, we're teaching them to take the responsibility that comes with it right into adulthood.

This concept of freedom leading up to being responsible can be explained in a short example. Kids love to splash in puddles. Now, as a parent, my first inclination is to tell them to go around the puddle, because I know that the splashing is going to cause wet clothes, which leads to a wet body, which leads to a little one complaining that it's cold. But when you let your kids have the freedom to play outdoors like kids do, they see firsthand the consequences of their decisions. That leads to understanding the responsibility that comes with the choices they make.

So when your child decides to splash in a puddle, they get to see how the water goes everywhere. Then they experience the cold with that water splashing on their clothes. Overall, they're learning that there are consequences to their actions and they're figuring out early on how to make responsible decisions. Do they want to splash and get wet, or do they want to save it for another day when getting wet isn't so bad?

There is another simple example of them making responsible decisions, when a child learns how to plant seeds and grow a garden, they see the fruit of their labor. They are learning that their actions can have good consequences, not just negative ones. These concepts were so appealing to my husband and me. We wanted our children to learn at an early age the consequences of their actions, both good and bad. We always thought of it like this: when you are young you have small choices with small consequences, but when you are older the choices and consequences grow with you and can easily impact the rest of your life. As the proverb says, "train up a child in the way (they) should go: and when (they are) old they will not depart far from it" We believe this applies first and most importantly training them on how to make decisions that are right for them and their circumstances. Marrying that philosophy with the other philosophy outlined in this book they will grow to be kind, empathetic and resilient adults. We wanted them to figure things out for themselves—although not everything, of course, because we recognize that there's a healthy balance that must be met. It's part of the idea that people learn by doing even with a struggle rather than by being told what to do (or not do), which is something I'll talk about in the next chapter.

Building a Self-Assured Identity

Letting our children play outside will ultimately provide powerful armor against peer pressure. One group of researchers performed a study of children of varying ages and their reactions to outdoor time. The study consisted of various tasks, or activities, done in nature, from following an animal trail to creating art from what they found in the forest. According to their findings, 84% of the 451 children surveyed said they felt more confident that they could do what they set their mind to accomplishing after the outdoor activities (Sheldrake et al., 2019). It is my opinion that children will conform to societal norms because they don't know any other way. When children don't know that they can do what makes them happy, they fall in line and do what they think is expected of them.

Sheldrake et al.'s (2019) study shows that once kids get outside and follow a challenging trail, build a shelter or fort, or navigate difficult terrain, they discover they can do the hard stuff. This builds inner strength and resilience, which boosts their confidence. Rather than "can't," they learn "can." The best part is that by not falling in line with what they think society expects, they also do not give in to peer pressure—one of the most debilitating factors for a kid navigating the world of their classmates and friends.

It's Just Right

There is a behavior that comes with hygge that we have tried to let our children fully experience. It is called *lagom*. This term reminds me of Goldilocks and the three bears. You know: too hot, too cold, or just right! *Lagom* is the idea that everything is just right. This behavior or idea promotes modesty and teamwork while discouraging extreme individuality. In other words, it's the fair thing to do or equality. It is related to hygge in that everything is in moderation. For example, you don't want to be a glutton and eat too much yummy cake, or when you want to have dinner with friends, it doesn't need to be a fancy, over-the-top affair.

I think it's important to cover *friluftsliv* and *lagom*, since I don't think you can talk about Danish parenting and hygge without these two concepts coming up. Honestly, all of them make it just right.

But the way I've explained *lagom* makes it almost too simple, and there's a bit more to it than that. *Lagom* is more of a Swedish principle, one that allows us to live a balanced life with little fuss. It is a state of being that we strive to achieve, since it allows us to be more happy, more centered, and better able to sustain equanimity in the face of the pressures of life.

According to the culture, *lagom* is a concept that promotes the idea that more than just enough is a waste of time. It goes along with ideals like selflessness, responsibility, and a belief in the common good. It almost feels like it would be a crime to exhibit excess in anything, because that might take away something that others might need.

What We Think About *Friluftsluv* and *Lagom*

The concept of *friluftsluv*, living an open-air life, and *lagom*, the just-enough life, are lifestyles that are not completely familiar to most of us. Within my culture, it feels like most children I know stay indoors due to living in the city and a familial preoccupation with excess. Parks in cities and towns are not as prevalent as they should be, and often they're not easily accessible if you don't have transportation.

However, part of what makes Danish parenting unique lies in the above-noted concepts. Children across the country can play outdoors, and families can roam wherever they would like. The country simply requests that people take care of the land, don't trespass on the little private property there is, and leave everything the way they found it. It's not a bad exchange for letting their kids play and learn so many life skills.

As parents, there are steps we can take to give our children the freedom they need for this outdoor play, even if it doesn't look exactly like what Danish families do. However, there are also things we can do with our kids that don't require going to a park or a forest. It's up to the individual family, and although one family's friluftsluv may not look the same as another's, that is fine. We each do what fits our family. Of course, I also like the idea of lagom. Asking my children to learn to take just what they needed so there's enough for everyone, has taught them a sense of thinking of others as well as responsibility. Since that is one of the traits I wanted to see in my children more than anything, I was happy to be consistent in teaching them these concepts.

Playtime Brings Life Growth and Overall Good Health

Playtime is important in Danish culture, and parents utilize indoor and outdoor play to foster key life skills such as empathy, problem solving, building character, integrity and more. Naturally, children love to play, and Danish parenting recognizes that they are learning while they are playing. Therefore, this chapter will first explain how to teach children to grow in empathy. Then, we'll talk about how kids gain negotiation skills, how we can have conversations with them to increase their awareness of themselves and others and these skills can all be strengthened through play. We will also touch on self-identification, how they are learning to self-govern and the benefits of having the habit of playing outdoors. Let's get to it!

The Learning Process: Empathy and Negotiation Through Play

As parents, we can talk at our children to tell them how life should be and what they should do in all situations. But let's be real; we all know that kids are inclined to learn from the "school of hard knocks." How many of us remember our parents grumbling about how we should have listened to their words of experience rather than learning life lessons the hard way?

However, I was quick to embrace the idea that my children could learn many life lessons through play. First and foremost in my mind was the idea that kids could learn how to interact with others, even if it was someone they didn't like. We all have to learn how to deal with people we don't like just as much as the ones we do get along with. That life lesson is not one our kids can learn simply by hearing what we have to say. Instead, they need to experience it firsthand, and the best way to do that is through play, when the consequences don't have to be so drastic.

Empathy Through Play

The natural question at this point is to ask exactly how our children are learning empathy during playtime. I mean, honestly, most parents—and I'm no exception—don't pay a lot of attention to what goes on when children play. We tune it out until, of course, our tiny loved ones do something over the top that drags our attention away from whatever we're doing to focus instead on their antics. Maybe a yelling match erupts between two children who have a difference of opinion about what's going to be done with that amazing fort they just built. Or, the fort gets destroyed because someone "isn't playing right," and there's a whole life lesson right there. But whatever happens, parents want to know what their kids are learning.

Here's the great thing. Playtime comes naturally to children, and their minds are constantly active and filled with ideas—maybe some great and some not-so-great. But this is where the fun begins, because children are taking these ideas and working with other kids about how to incorporate all the ideas into whatever game they've got going on. Once kids get into the thick of the game—putting together the rules and figuring out how the games will work—all they see are other kids. They're not looking for kids who think like them, or look like them, or are from the same social class. What they're looking for are ideas: how to make the game or the fort the best it can be.

Here are a few more examples of ways children play that encourage and teach empathy. Children love the world of pretend, and there is nothing I love more than hearing words like "Pretend you're a princess and I'm a dragon" when listening to kids play—especially when it turned out that the princess was going to be played by the boy next door while my daughter was the dragon. I think one of the most important ways to learn how to be empathetic is to take on a role that is not a societal norm. When kids step into role-playing with the idea that they're going to pretend to be someone that society doesn't expect, they are learning empathy for others. When my daughter pretended to be a dragon, she went against society's ideas that, as a girl, she should be a "helpless" princess needing to be rescued from the dragon. The neighbor boy never argued with my daughter when she wanted him to have the part of the girl during their play. He became very empathetic toward the role of girls in society, and I believe it happened through playtime.

Playtime for children is filled with "Pretend you're..." lines, and I've listened to kids pretending to be superheroes, villains, animals, gods and goddesses, inanimate objects, cartoon characters, and sometimes family members. One of the best things about these pretend-play games is that children are stepping into roles that they are interested in or they're trying to figure out. This type of play allows them to place themselves in situations that they want to learn how to handle; sometimes the outcome isn't what we'd expect, but they're all learning moments for the kids. And, what are they learning? How to be empathetic.

I love being part of or just observing this pretend play. It shows me, in the best way, how my children are learning. Through observation, I begin to see how my kids comprehend roles and behaviors. When I join in the play, I am able to use it as a teaching moment. Without calling it that, I can introduce roles and behaviors that are encouraged.

Children are learning to be empathetic toward others, but what if they can't figure out what someone is feeling? There is a great game that kids enjoy that will teach them how to figure out how someone is feeling based on their actions, especially if the child cannot recognize the emotion based on facial expressions. By using a facial expression while acting out the emotion associated with it, children can learn to observe behaviors to learn about the emotions of others. In case you haven't figured it out, I'm talking about charades, and this is a game that you can initiate at home to help children learn what an emotion looks like on someone else. I always felt like my kids learned so much more than just how to recognize emotions when we played charades; they were really getting the picture about how people can express the same emotion in a different way.

For instance, a friend of mine withdraws when she is upset or feels sad. She isn't comfortable with outward expressions of sympathy. She doesn't cry or show any of the usual ways of expressing sadness that my kids were most familiar with. However, teaching our kids that there is another way that people can show they are sad helped them recognize and ultimately embrace the differences they saw in everyone.

The Art of Negotiation Through Play

Children learn how to negotiate through play, as well. I have listened to my children negotiate their way through a board game, especially Monopoly, as well as outdoor play. I think empathy plays a bit into the idea of negotiation, but as I mentioned earlier, children need to learn how to get along with others even if they don't view things the same way. Outdoor play, being one type of play in particular, is one of the best ways for kids to learn this art.

Children love to build forts, sand castles on the beach, roads for their trucks in the dirt, and sometimes construction projects like bike ramps. Anything that a child can think of, they usually want to build. So where does negotiation come in? Well, as my siblings, friends and I learned, you can't just throw up a couple pieces of plywood and say it's a working treehouse or fort. There are elements of design, especially for a treehouse. I mean, the tree is the number one part of any treehouse, but to build a fun but safe one, there are a lot of factors to take into account. Children understand this, often by past experience. So when children get together and decide to construct a fort of some kind, all ideas are on the table and from there, children learn to negotiate and even compromise during the building process.

When faced with a decision about construction, children are also learning effective problem-solving. Maybe one of the kids had a grand idea about how to build the thing and everyone agreed, so they tried it. It almost worked, but not quite. So all the kids went back to the drawing board, with each child trying to come up with a new solution.

Each child will have a role and a responsibility that they apply to the project; through this type of play, kids will learn how to navigate the intricacies of social interactions. Shared experiences will give them the chance to truly understand each other. But what they're doing is refining the ability to effectively communicate while learning how to resolve conflicts with grace and, you guessed it, empathy.

Following the Rules: Understanding How Rules Work Through Play

Children need rules. As we've discussed, they don't need the rules crammed down their throat or to be given ultimatums if one is broken, but rules help children understand how the world works. Children play all kinds of games with rules: hide and seek, tag, board games, cards, sporting events, and more. As a parent, how often have you heard your kids discuss the rules of a game, sometimes even changing the rules a little? Believe it or not, this is a vital part of social interaction since it helps children learn how to share and how to take turns (Whitebread et al., 2012). Honestly, they're also learning how to understand the world through another perspective. How old were you when you realized you could tell how someone navigates the world based on how they follow, or don't follow, the rules of a game? Playing games that have set rules can tell you a lot about a person, and children are good at studying the character of another person.

Children will also make up their own games and amazingly enough, these new games always have rules. Kids are very aware that games have rules, and my experience has taught me that it's a rare child who throws caution to the wind and comes up with a game that has no guidelines. As I have seen in my children who love to create games, especially ones they use their imagination to explore new roles and abilities. One game they were creating had just one rule, make up a character that you can do whatever you want with it. For my kids those games don't last long and they don't go back to them.

Growth Within Play: The Art of Perception

Teaching our children the art of perception helps them look into situations by observing and understanding the world around them. Through conversations about their play time we can help them develop an empathic eye to better understand their roles in play and the friendships they are building during play time. Through play and conversation with us as parents, children can learn to be observant, understanding, patient and a better friend. Which ultimately creates a more confident, capable and independent adult.

Here's a hypothetical example that should explain this concept more clearly. A few children are building towers out of blocks and in general playing near each other, but each child is building individually. One of the children notices another child whose tower keeps falling, because the child is struggling with balancing the blocks properly. The child who is watching sees that the other one begins to cry after their tower has collapsed for the third time.

The observing child realizes that the other child is sad and probably becoming frustrated. They scoot closer to the other and offer aid, and together they build the tower, with one child showing the other how to position the blocks so they are balanced and will not fall over.

This is a hypothetical scenario, but it explains one of the ways I worked with my children. I did a bit of guided work with them. We observed and problem-solved together, trying to think creatively and come up with ways to help others. But ultimately, it's an experiment I did with them to put them in each other's shoes. I asked how they would feel if certain situations were happening to them. It built their perception of a situation by asking them to take on the problem themselves, and it worked well with my kids.

The Journey to Morals: Exploring Values and Beliefs

When children play with other kids, their character can sometimes be challenged. They are going to play with kids who don't agree with their ideas or who don't share the same values or belief system. Childhood is a time for kids to figure out their values and beliefs based on everything they learn at home, and this influences their actions toward others. So when those values get challenged during play, they have the opportunity to examine and validate them through how they interact and respond to others.

The example I have here is a bit extreme, but it effectively explains what I'm trying to say in this section.

Some of the neighborhood children are outside playing a game when a lone child comes up and asks to join. One of the kids has always shown signs of being a bully and takes control of the situation, loudly asserting his "authority" and verbally pushing the new kid around. He begins to change the rules of the game to showcase his strengths and intimidate the newcomer. A couple of the other kids are too afraid to speak up and they stay quiet, going along with whatever the bully says. But there are a couple of kids in the group who do not like or approve of this behavior.

They try to be diplomatic and reset the game back to the correct rules without causing embarrassment or shame to anyone, but they're prepared to stand firm against the bully if necessary.

I know that it's extreme, but there will always be bullies in life and it's a valuable lesson when our children learn to speak up about their beliefs and morals. It is also a life lesson to the kids, because they've learned how to calmly and rationally overcome a difficulty without letting it escalate into something that could be avoided. My son likes online gaming, and I know that bullying behavior can be found within that medium, as well.

Within our family, I often have conversations with my kids about what happened during playtime. These talks provided a safe space where they felt comfortable telling me stuff that happened, what they said or did, and how they felt about it. They knew I would listen and praise the behavior that we taught them was right, along with validating their feelings. But they also knew I would work with them to adjust the behavior that didn't align with what we taught.

Lessons in Loss: Navigating Difficult Emotions Through Play

As we've discussed, children take their cue from their parents for everything, from joy to anger to sorrow and loss. Of course, there is more than one type of loss. Maybe mom or dad worked hard for a promotion at work, but they didn't get it, or one parent lost their job. Or, of course, the first thing we think of when we hear loss: the death of a loved one, either a pet or a human.

Although children use their parents as a reference for how to deal with a loss, they take that foundation and apply it to their make-believe games. Within the scenarios they create, children will try out various ways of approaching loss to determine which one suits them the best.

Then, there's the real-world reaction to loss. Your child comes across a bird with an injured wing while playing outside, or they discover a small animal that has been left dead on the doorstep by the family cat. Our goal with the Danish style of parenting was to raise emotionally intelligent children, and these instances helped shape their emotional patterns. Situations like these offer powerful teaching moments with the opportunity to navigate the complex emotions that arise. Empathy, compassion, loss—your child feels it all.

Fortunately, you've been raising your child to embrace their own decisions and to take action that is dependent on understanding the situation instead of reacting to an intense emotion. Everything children do and experience builds the adults they become. They need to learn how to process deep emotions without giving in to base instincts or reactions.

I've listened to my children during their make-believe playtime and it has caused me to stop and pay attention to what's going on. Children learn early on that life is not a fairytale and happy endings aren't always the outcome, and they learn how to work through their disappointment or grief as they strengthen their life skills. When children go through a loss, witness the death of a pet, or hear their parents talk about job loss—whatever is happening in their world—they incorporate those experiences into play. Their make-believe becomes dark or the sunny stories become tragedies, but how they manipulate the players will tell you how they're dealing with the loss.

Self-Identification: Early Autonomy Through Play

Playtime teaches a child their self-worth, preferences, strengths, and quirks. When they engage in their pretend worlds, they are molding their sense of identity. Encouraging this creative exploration in the world of make-believe will ensure that your child has autonomy, which is what makes probably the biggest impact on their lives. Autonomy is a basic human need and is "essential to individual well-being, motivation, and psychological health" (Cherry, 2023a). Through play, as your child begins to determine their identity and actions, a sense of control is developed. They are starting to understand that they control their destiny, which becomes a determining factor in their future work and academic goals.

Autonomy means that your child will know they can take control of their life and steer it toward their chosen destiny, rather than feeling like a pawn being moved about by other people or forces beyond their control. When a child plays pretend—building worlds or making decisions about events that take place—they are aligning their preferences, behaviors, needs, and motivations. In the worlds they create, the child feels they're living a life that coincides with their interests rather than the will of someone else.

I want to be clear there is a difference between role playing online and playing pretend in a physical space with others. I have seen too many kids and adults lose themselves in these online role playing games when they think they can pretend to be whoever they want to be. In the online games they can also be easily influenced by others who do not have the children's best interest at heart. The real life pretend and play is what I am talking about that will bring this life growth we all desire children to achieve.

The Magic of Outdoor Activities: Enhancing Well-Being

We probably all heard our parents say, "Go play outside, it's good for you," and while we may not have realized it as children, they were simply repeating what the American Academy of Pediatrics (AAP) and health professionals have promoted. As a parent, our goal is to raise mentally and physically healthy children. Genetics aside, outdoor play promotes a healthier lifestyle.

The AAP strongly advocates for more time spent in active play, emphasizing that it is essential for the physical, mental, and social well-being of children. This aligns with the Danish parenting style and their outdoor learning philosophy that I discussed in the last chapter. According to the AAP, active play during early childhood lays the foundation for a healthy lifestyle throughout life (American Academy of Pediatrics, 2018).

Dr. Robert Murray, a member of the AAP, highlights that regular physical activity for children does the following:

- Promotes healthy growth and development

- Enhances cognitive function

- Reduces the risk of obesity and other chronic conditions

Moreover, the AAP emphasizes that reducing screen time and ensuring adequate sleep are just as crucial as promoting active play. This holistic approach resonates with parents seeking to improve the health and well-being of their children.

Pediatricians Dr. Danette Glassy and Dr. Pooja Tandon (2022) offer suggestions for outdoor play, and I will give further specifics and examples of that outdoor play in the final chapter of this book. But they give us clear reasons for promoting outdoor play as well as its specific benefits. They do not all have to do with health, but also relate to the overall well-being of children.

The most obvious is improved physical health, which means lower obesity rates and improved motor development. Children's mental health improves with outdoor play as well. Children with better mental health have lower levels of stress and depression. Outdoor play also increases the positive behavior of children so they have less anger and aggression and decreases symptoms in children with ADHD. Their impulse control is kept in check more easily. Children who spend a lot of time playing outside also have a higher interest in learning. The fresh air activities that are so good for them increase blood flow to the brain, which builds their creativity, curiosity, and critical thinking.

I understand that this portion of the chapter on play is a little more scientific, but sometimes it's helpful to scientifically back up the decisions we make within our lifestyles. Often, children and people will find it easier to be less critical about something they don't understand when they can see more than just us as parents saying it.

My son is a perfect example of using science to help him understand the "why" we did not approve of certain games and movies until he reached certain ages. He accepted that we didn't want him to spend hours on games but wanted to know why, rather than saying it was just because "I said so" we talked with him about what we learned from other sources. For media we have used a resource like commonsensemedia.org that gives a description of what is in the media and other parents, kids and a nonpartial 3rd party share their input about the particular media. This helped us avoid him starting movies and games like Minecraft and Roblox for years! This same tactic helps us be more educated and answer questions like how much sleep does a child really need, why should I eat my vegetables, why do I need to do math? The point is, you are not alone and there are many online resources to help you have these conversations!

A friend of mine with grown children always says that she is so much more relaxed about her kids and their lives because she knows their emotional and physical well-being is in good shape. She has a decreased sense of anxiety and stress when she thinks about her kids because she knows that they can handle anything that comes their way. They may call her for advice or just to talk, but she knows that whatever happens, they've already dealt with the situation. It is so freeing to know that our children are out there in the world equipped with the tools they need to survive mentally, emotionally, and physically.

Ultimately, learning empathy, negotiation, responsibility, self-governance, and how to deal with loss through childhood play lasts into adulthood. The idea of learning these things through the simple act of playtime seems like such a small thing, but really, what you are helping your child learn is how to successfully and confidently navigate relationships. Your child will have the ability to connect with others with a level of understanding that they have gained from becoming empathetic. The lessons learned in childhood will become a lasting, vital part of their lives, allowing them to build strong friendships, collaborate effectively with others in the work field, and build harmonious family bonds. In other words, your children will learn how to excel in the world because they are driven by empathy and understanding.

Hopefully, the outdoor play that your child enjoys during their childhood will continue into adulthood and play an important role in their overall physical and mental health. It's easy to focus on the emotional health of our children, especially since we know that so much of what happens in life can negatively impact their emotional well-being, but it's so important to remember that the physical health of a person can have an impact on their mental health. By giving our children playtime, and especially outdoor play, we are improving both.

Parenting Begins With You

This chapter discusses you, the parent, and what your role will be. The primary goal is to describe the mindset you will need as you start thinking about adopting Danish parenting practices. Let's be honest, we're probably all interested in the Danish parenting style because it sounds so lovely and is so different from our own childhood experiences. More importantly, we want to know if it's something we can do. Right now, you may even be wondering if it's something you're ready to do.

No matter what parenting style we choose to follow, navigating parenthood can be tricky. Too often, we experience detours that feel as though they will wipe out the progress we've made. To help overcome that danger, there is a very important piece of advice that will enable us to maneuver around even the worst of the potholes on this road we are traveling.

This parenting journey starts with you. You have decided to branch out in a new direction and to follow an unexplored path. The Danish parenting style may not be new, but it is new to you, your family, and maybe even your culture. Some of the concepts or ideas we've touched on so far may seem unusual to you, and maybe you're a little nervous about whether or not it's something you can do. But what you do know is that somehow, your children's lives need to be different than what you experienced as a child.

This chapter will set down some ground rules to make your adjustment to this style of parenting easier. Although some of the concepts may seem out of reach, this is a parenting style that you can absolutely embrace if you so choose; remember, what will feel awkward in the beginning will start to become natural to you over time.

Fostering Empathy, Kindness, and Social Skills

Children depend on their parents, and most of them still believe we have their best interests at heart. It is best if we learn to empathize with our children's emotions and validate their experiences. Empathy is the ability to understand and share another person's feelings. It is important to understand what they are struggling with and how it affects them. This can help you tune in to their emotions and show that you understand and accept them. It's also important to acknowledge your own emotions, as it can be hard to show empathy if you're frustrated or upset. Validation is the act of acknowledging and accepting someone's feelings as valid. When validating a child's feelings, it's important to acknowledge how they're feeling without judgment or comment on what they "should" be feeling. This can help create a safe space for them to express their emotions without fear of judgment. Validation is about listening and letting them know you hear them, rather than trying to fix the situation right away. Both empathy and validation can be important when interacting with children, and can help build stronger relationships. By learning to empathize and see our children from their point of view, we can help them grow in kindness, confidence and better understand the world around them. Remember, even if children don't always obey perfectly, they will still eventually mimic our behavior for better or for worse. So we need to ask, what is that behavior that they're going to imitate? It might help you to remember they will mirror you in the following ways:

- When we communicate to our children that we see their side of a situation they learn to see our side.

- When we set expectations and then offer the support they need to reach what is asked of them they will want to do it. We don't leave them to figure it out themselves; we provide them with the tools as well as support they need to succeed.

- When we practice what we preach they will follow our example.

- When we truly listen to our children to understand they learn the value of true friendships and what it is like to be heard and understood.

- When we show how delighted we are by them, they learn what traits they have that bring joy to others and increase their confidence and self esteem.

- When we forgive their mistakes and relate to them they learn nobody is perfect—but they also learn they are perfect just the way they are.

- When we apologize and make amends for our mistakes they learn how to repair the damage they've done with their mistakes.

- When we say no to a request but still offer understanding they learn that they don't always get what they want. However, they do have what they need the most, which is parents who are there for them.

On the other hand, though, remember that

- When we spank them for wrongdoing, they learn that people with power can hit those who are weaker.

- When we promise to do something with them but then back out of it, they learn that it's okay to break a promise.

- When we scream at our kids, they learn that temper tantrums are okay and we're teaching them to scream at us.

- When we lie, they learn that dishonesty is okay.

- When we punish them, they learn that they're bad.

One of the most important things parents can remember is that it is not harsh discipline or punishment that teaches our children right from wrong. It is the adults in their lives —their parents—showing them through everyday actions how to be responsible, generous, honest, compassionate, and empathetic. Experience has taught me that children will not always make the right choices, but we can raise children who want to make the right decisions. Ultimately we want to see our children making the right choices on their own because they want to, not because they feel like they should. Instead of lecturing our children to act a certain way, let it come from how we live our life as well as how they feel we think about who they are and what they might become.

Be Authentic

I believe authenticity is one of the most important aspects of parenting. My husband and I have found that we are most authentic when we stay true to our personalities, values, and spirit—what we call our inner compass. This inner compass is an authentic self-esteem that guides us toward a sense of peace, happiness, and joy. I remember introducing the concept to our youngest during a special family gathering. We prepped the kids in advance, letting them know we were going to talk about something extra special. That evening, we went to a Mexican restaurant and spent time together discussing what we value, how to recognize and understand our feelings—both good and bad—and how to act in a way that aligns with our values and core beliefs.

Because we had prepared the children for the conversation, it became a memorable and meaningful experience for all of us. Staying true to our core beliefs, even when under pressure to act otherwise, allows us to live authentically. And in doing so, we show our children how to be their authentic selves as well. Being honest with ourselves and with others, including admitting our mistakes, can be challenging, especially as parents. But when we demonstrate authenticity with our children, it will have a lasting impact, in both how they act as well as feel towards themselves and others. It will also build bonds of trust and respect. We want them to see that we stand up for our values and live with integrity because we believe that they will learn more from our example than from anything else.

I have also noticed how authentic praise to our children have improved our relationship and feelings towards each other. Another thing we remember to do is focus on the positive aspects of our child's behavior, rather than the negative. In letting my children know when they have worked hard on something and praising the effort rather then the results, builds a sense of accomplishment that will build their self-esteem. My little girl just the other day smiled up at me and said "mom I love it when you talk to me that way." I have had special moments time after time when I take the time to talk with my children about how well they are behaving and doing.

Understand Respect and Practice Respectful Communication

Being authentic leads to mutual respect and trust between you and your children. Within many families, the idea of respect is something children were expected to show adults simply because they were grown-ups. A few ways to define respect: to admire someone or something because of their abilities, qualities and/or achievements. To have regard for someone's feelings, wishes and rights. You accept someone for who they are even when they are different or you don't agree with them.

But for children to understand the concept of respect, we need to look at it another way. The bottom line is that we'll be teaching our kids to treat others how they want to be treated, and hopefully, they will learn how to treat others by observing our behavior. So we want to show them the kind of behavior to focus on. There are two parts of respect to explain to children.

First, we want our children to be happy and even a little proud of how their words and actions make themselves and others feel. Second, we want our children to care enough about others to duplicate the behavior that allows other people to feel as happy as the child has felt when they are treated well.

That means my husband and I show respect to our children by being careful with what we say and how we treat them so they never feel undervalued or unappreciated. As they've grown, we have seen how that same sense of respect is reflected in how they treat others. I now use the acronym T.H.I.N.K. when I talk about respect with my children. We've all been told to "think before we speak," here the T.H.I.N.K. acronym stands for:

- **T**rue: Is it true?

- **H**elpful: Is it helpful?

- **I**nspiring: Is it inspiring?

- **N**ecessary: Is it necessary?

- **K**ind: Is it kind?

Unless all of the above are true, then don't say whatever you were thinking about (Koons, 2019). Just because something is true does not mean we need to say it. True things can be said that are not helpful, and it may feel like the truth at the moment but later we may find it wasn't all true. Likewise we need to be aware that what we are saying may not inspire another and so it just may not be necessary, or kind. Sadly, I and many others have said rude things to one another more than once, and I want that kind of behavior to change in my own life and I know it starts with me. When you T.H.I.N.K. about what you say, you're better able to:

- take control of your thoughts

- make good decisions

- talk less

- listen more

When our children learn they can trust us to be considerate of how they feel and their opinions, they will extend that same trust back to us. This creates mutual respect in our relationship, since trust follows respect.

We've mentioned open communication when it comes to the Danish parenting style, but we must also remember that it still needs to be respectful. Being respectful in our communication means paying attention to what our children have to say. It doesn't mean that we lay down the law and then expect them to have no thoughts about what we've dictated.

We cannot expect our children to respect our decisions or our ideas unless we show that we are willing to consider their input. The Danish family is not run as a dictatorship, with the parents issuing commands for the rest of the family to blindly follow. It is not the type of household where the parents tell the children they must accept a decision "because I said so." Those types of behaviors leave children feeling powerless and quite frankly, unappreciated.

An example of my children having a say, which many parents would not have allowed, involved the walk to a friend's house one morning. We once lived in an area that got a lot of rain, and it had rained the night before and was still a bit drizzly that morning as we got ready. It was about a 7-minute walk to the friend's house. My youngest was dressed and putting her stuff in her bag. She grabbed her favorite jacket off the back of the chair and her rain jacket fell on the floor. Without thinking I picked up the rain jacket and told her to take that one. She asked, "Why? This one is my favorite," and held up the other one. I explained to her that it was supposed to rain that day and she would want the rain jacket if they played outside. She thought for just a second, then said, "Okay," and exchanged jackets without disagreement.

I thought another disagreement would start, though, when I told her to get her umbrella for the walk. She said she didn't want it. I told her to put on the rain jacket then. She said that she'd rather go without. So I calmly explained to her that if she chose not to take the umbrella or put on her rain jacket and it started raining hard on the way to her friends, she was going to get wet. She said she understood, so I asked how she would feel if she got wet. Her answer to that was that she would just take her raincoat out of the bag and put it on if she needed to. Our conversation was pleasant and I meant it when I told her to let me know how it worked out. I want my kids to know that I truly care about their decisions and the results of those choices.

I gave her the freedom to choose because it was a minor battle and I learned early on to pick my battles. Had it been a cold winter day with snow on the ground, there would not have been any disagreement about whether she wore a jacket or not—that's a choice I would have chosen, for her health and safety.

Children are quick learners and they understand much more than we give them credit for. When we take the time to explain the thought process behind the rules to our children, they can see where we're coming from. But remember, they are looking at the world through fresh eyes and they might have something to say that could change how we see things. Giving our children an option is important, but it's also important that they understand the consequences of their decision. For example, no jacket means the possibility of being cold and wet at her friends.

There is nothing wrong with changing or adjusting your viewpoint since a good debate provides an opportunity for one side to persuade the other to change their thinking, even if only partially. As an adult, I have often found myself holding tight to an opinion or idea simply because I'm not willing to change my mind. But I have also discovered that if I give the other person a chance to talk about it, I will often loosen up and adjust my stance. It doesn't mean I was wrong; most of the time it simply means that I was too set in my ways to see another side to the situation or to recognize that I was holding on to some past hurt. We are all learning to be respectful of one another's choices as well as to trust that we have each other's best interests in mind.

Be Consistent

One of the worst things about being a child is when the adults in your life are not consistent. It's not just when they're inconsistent with rules; it's when they decide they're going to change how they react or they're going to implement some new way of doing something. Everything is great for a week or two until they decide it's too hard or it's not working, and suddenly everything goes back to the way it was before—usually not in the kids' favor, either.

Inconsistency leaves a child feeling adrift, helpless, and frustrated. Most of the time we, as parents, are going to experience backlash in the form of temper tantrums or "I hate you!" when we have tried to push our will onto our children rather than allow them the chance to speak their minds. Unfortunately, it's too easy to push our will onto our kids when it feels like what we are doing is not working.

Sometimes, in the beginning, it felt too hard to have an open dialogue with my kids because I thought they were just being silly or saying things to see how I would react. I was often tired, and between my husband getting upset because he just wanted the kids to do what they were told and the kids being kids, I sometimes wondered if it would be easier to go back to the way I was raised.

It took a lot of effort on my part to stay calm and keep to the path I'd chosen. I knew the rewards would be so much greater if I could just keep my temper and my impatience in check. In the beginning, it was also difficult to keep the voices of my parents and other adults out of my head. Since it took a while for them to come around to my choice to adopt the Danish parenting style, they had a lot to say about how we were raising our children. Family visits almost always became hostile skirmishes and honestly, those were the times I was ready to give up the most. I had not been raised to go against the adults in my life and I would always be a child to my parents.

However, it was also in these challenging moments that my desire grew stronger. I remembered how it felt as a child when I wasn't heard, when my voice seemed to get lost, and I knew I couldn't do that to my own kids. So, no matter how tough it gets, stay consistent! It's tempting to shift gears when things feel overwhelming, but changing the rules all the time will confuse your kids and make things harder in the long run. The real payoff of consistency shows up when it matters most—like during those tough days when life feels chaotic, and you can't give your full attention. The behaviors you have worked on have become second nature to your kids. I think back to the effort it took to teach our kids how to behave in church. We talked about it over and over—why it's important to act a certain way and how we wanted to respect the service. Now, when I see them doing what we've discussed, without a single reminder, it's like this huge sigh of relief. All that time being consistent, into reminding and correcting them, paid off, and we enjoy the time together that much more.

I recommend that you start small. Honestly, the degree of change you are looking to make and the result you're hoping for will determine the challenge to your family. So I would say learn your family's dynamics and then work toward your goal by making changes in small increments. Work within the parameters of your family's personalities. Don't make a change because someone else is doing it or someone you know reads it in a book. The goal is to gain the education you need to implement small changes in a manner that your family can accept and work with.

Set Rules and Consequences With No Ultimatums

As stated in earlier chapters, there will always be a need for rules, and Danish families don't just throw all the rules out the window. Children are taught the value of following rules both in school and at home, and they learn the natural consequences of breaking those rules. With that in mind, it's important to understand the difference between consequences, punishments, and ultimatums.

Consequences

This may be a simplified definition, but the consequences need to match the crime, so to speak. For example, if you throw something, it gets taken away.

It is good to let your children know there are positive consequences as well. Yes, we want our children to understand the consequences of poor decision-making, but we also want them to recognize that consequences is not just a negative word. A pleasant consequence can be the result of good decision-making. For example, if my children stayed focused and got ready for bed without dawdling or complaining, we read an extra story.

The bottom line is that our children need to understand they are capable of taking responsibility for their choices and can handle the outcome.

Punishment

Punishments usually involve some sort of yelling, spanking, or withholding affection. It is illegal in Denmark to spank a child, since it leaves the children feeling depressed, devalued, and with little self-worth. Spanking also promotes lying in children, because they will do whatever they can to avoid corporal punishment.

Unfortunately, there is more to punishment than just the physical aspect like hitting. Withholding affection is an emotional punishment, which can be just as devastating to the child and can cause the same problems as spanking.

The silent treatment was something a close friend of mine endured quite frequently as a child, and it caused emotional damage as she got older. Even today, as an adult, she struggles when people do not respond to her. The emotional violence caused by any kind of withholding affection is a real struggle and extremely damaging.

As you can see, punishment and utilizing fear ultimately are not the most effective tools to get children to behave well. Instead, we want them to understand the natural consequences of their actions and decisions. This impacts the next choice they must make when figuring out the right thing to do.

Ultimatums

Ultimatums are threats. For example, the ultimatum "If you don't eat everything on your plate, you'll sit at the table until you do. If you don't eat it before bedtime, you'll have it for breakfast," was something my husband heard often as a child. He remembers on one occasion, he curled up on the bench seat and fell asleep at the table.

Punishments and ultimatums are power struggles to keep the adult in control of the children.

There is something to keep in mind about children, though. Remember how I mentioned earlier that Danish parents don't view children as bad? Instead, they believe they are Inherently good and treat them accordingly. Rather than calling it the "terrible twos," they call that age the "boundary age" and they consider pushing boundaries to be normal. The concept is welcome in their society. People grow by pushing boundaries, and the Danish people believe this is how children figure out life. Therefore, they embrace this part of their child's life.

It comes down to how we need to teach our children that there are always consequences for our actions, and I want to reiterate that these can be both positive and negative. The term "consequences" should not be associated with only something negative. In my mind, the most important part is for our children to learn to recognize what the consequences will be, so they are better equipped to make their choices.

Be Honest and Teach Honesty

Honesty is the best policy and should extend to our relationship with our kids. We need to be truthful about how we feel about stuff that happens. We're asking them to be forthright with us, but how can they learn to do that if we aren't authentic with them? Granted, there is some emotional baggage we carry around that we don't need to unload on our kids, but they do need to know when something hurts us or makes us scared. We want to be superheroes to our kids, but I'd say that there's something superhero-like about being vulnerable as well. Here are some tips for teaching honesty to your kids as well as expressing it yourself:

- Express your thoughts and feelings when it is appropriate.

- Give your kids honest, age-appropriate answers to their questions.

- Let your kids know that what they feel is normal—tell them stories from your childhood about the difficult times and the fun times.

- Be non-judgmental—put the focus on honesty over punishment.

- Teach children that they are the best they can be and there is no need for comparison with anyone else.

To wrap up this chapter, most of the time when we decide to take action toward a goal, we figure there's going to be a list of actions to take. But we don't talk about what we have to change within ourselves to reach that goal. I know; that sounds complicated, like it's a pretty difficult challenge. But it's not. It's simply a different mindset, and once we understand what we want, it will bring about a fundamental shift in ourselves.

Honestly, change comes from the realization that we want to become better at creating a genuine, kind, authentic relationship with other humans, especially our kids. It's about being more aware, kind, and patient as you work through self-development and self-growth.

Sometimes it's not as simple as changing the color of our walls or getting new furniture. Sometimes we have to change our entire foundation. This is what we're doing as parents when we embark on our journey toward adopting the Danish parenting style. We need to set up a new foundation and then build from there to become a better you.

I have a scenario for you to think about:

You are holding a cup of coffee when someone comes along and bumps into you or shakes your arm, making you spill your coffee everywhere.

Why did you spill the coffee?

You say because someone bumped into me!!!

Wrong answer.

You spilled the coffee because there was coffee in your cup.

Had there been tea in the cup, you would have spilled tea.

Whatever is inside the cup is what will spill out.

Therefore, when life comes along and shakes you (which WILL happen), whatever is inside you will come out. It's easy to fake it, until you get rattled.

So, we have to ask ourselves... What is in my cup?

When life gets tough, what spills over?

Joy, gratefulness, peace and humility?

Anger, bitterness, harsh words and reactions?

Life provides the cup, YOU choose how to fill it.

Today, let's work towards filling our cups with gratitude, forgiveness, joy, words of affirmation, as well as kindness, gentleness and love for others.

I think it is important to also remember that when the coffee spills out of your cup, the coffee doesn't just burn you, it burns the other people around you that it lands on. You have an unspoken social responsibility to make sure that your cup is full of something that doesn't burn and harm others.

Making your home a better place starts with you and what you decide to put in your cup will make a world of difference.

How a Child's Brain Works

Are you ready to dive in and talk about the child's brain? This chapter will do just that and share how an understanding of the brain helps us guide our children toward the life we dream of them living. Since the brain determines who we are and what we do, the goal is to learn how your child can use their whole brain. We want to help our children build a sturdy foundation for strong health in multiple areas:

- social

- mental

- emotional

When they use the whole brain, children will be better at the following:

- making decisions

- self-discipline

- self-awareness

- healthy relationships

Their Brain Will Mirror Us

According to Siegel and Bryson (2011) in their book *The Whole-Brain Child*, while our kids develop and grow, their brains mirror ours. So as we work on our own mental and emotional health, the happiness and stability that it brings about will transfer to our children's brains. Therefore, if we continue to grow and increase our own understanding, our children will do the same. However, it is also important to note that if we choose not to experience this personal growth, our children will suffer from that lack of insight. Remember, our kids mimic what we do and according to science, this includes brain us e.

Change Your Perception

One of the most important aspects of understanding how your child's brain works begins with you, the parent. To better understand how your children think and to recognize what they need from you, it's vital to start with you. The first thing you need to do is to change your perception. This is also called reframing, which is a huge part of Danish parenting. It's a way to place a higher importance on the positive instead of the negative. For example, rather than viewing a rainy day as cold and miserable, look at it as a way to stay indoors for a cozy time with the family while the outdoors gets a makeover. Alternatively, if you are like my husband, he feels it's a great opportunity to weed and do certain yard work as the kids splash in the rain.

This idea of reframing can be the key to happiness. This technique takes what could be negative and turns it into something positive. Yes, negativity is a part of life that we cannot escape, but focusing on the good instead of the bad whenever possible is one way to promote your children's well-being. Happiness doesn't necessarily come from the way things are, but instead, it comes from the way we view them. How do we see things—from a pessimistic or optimistic view? Can we see the silver lining when we look at something negative? Reframing makes us consider how we approach conflict, negativity, or difficult situations: with a glass half-full or glass half-empty mindset?

I remember, as a child, being told by every adult in my family that I was "too sensitive" and they even brought it up with other adults where I could hear them. I still think that it means there's something wrong with me, especially since my older brothers always told me I needed to "toughen up." Because of this, I view being sensitive as a flaw in my character. Anytime I cried, I was "too sensitive." If I didn't understand a joke made at my expense and I didn't laugh, I was "too sensitive." As I got older, the phrase "You have no sense of humor" went along with it.

The Danish parenting style does not include labeling your children. It is their opinion, and I agree, that there can be serious repercussions when these labels are affixed to our children, especially when we start diagnosing our children with psychological and neurological disorders. These labels can be especially damaging in school, where being in "special" classes follows kids around for the rest of their school days.

Within the new parenting style you've adopted, it's important to separate the person from the problem. Try to understand why a kid has bullying tendencies, or help your child understand why they feel a certain way. Don't tell them they should not feel the way they do; we are all entitled to our feelings and you've been helping your child to recognize and relate how they feel. Instead, figure out what's happening to make those feelings come out.

While reframing can be a very important tool for parenting, it's important to put a lot of thought into it and do some reading. Research this idea, because reframing can help you and your child see the world in a better, happier light. We will explore more about the child's brain later, but in the meantime, here are some tips.

Tip 1: Set an Example

Find a way to be more positive about life situations. Concentrate on separating the person from the action when you're upset with someone. Maybe a coworker was difficult to deal with that day and pointed out every mistake you made. Rather than chalk it up as them being rude, try to put yourself in their shoes. What could have happened to make them so nitpicky? Did they argue with someone at home, or did your boss pick apart their work? Try to see the other person's side of the situation.

Tip 2: Reframe Your Words

Rather than saying "I hate so-and-so," try to focus on a good part of their personality and say that instead. For example, rather than "I hate my neighbor," say "I like how well-tended my neighbor's yard always is."

Tip 3: Rewrite Your Child's Negative Qualities

Find words to describe your child that will focus on the positive side of their behavior. This will help you appreciate the uniqueness that is your child. For example, it was too easy for me to compare my children, since the oldest was always well-behaved and generally did not give me any problems. My youngest, though, was active and very energetic. I was exhausted just trying to get through day-to-day activities with her. I had to learn early on to focus on her zest for life and how that energy translated into happiness. Once I was able to do that, I discovered that it was easier to navigate everyday occurrences with my children since I stopped viewing things in a negative light.

Once you start finding the good in others or in bad situations, it will come naturally—and best of all, your children will start doing it, too. Remember, though, you have to find the good in yourself as well.

Survive and Thrive

Sometimes, as parents, we have days that make us feel like all we can do is survive. It feels next to impossible to get through one more day of our children being disrespectful, fighting between siblings, and the general chaos that surrounds kids when they feel a little out of control. We want to throw in the towel and give up, because these young ones are driving us crazy and we're not sure survival is going to work. Overall, though, we all want our children to be caring, compassionate, responsible, intelligent, confident adults who work hard and can participate in meaningful relationships.

The ultimate goal is for our kids to be

- happy

- independent

- successful

To achieve these goals for our children, parents can learn to take the challenging times and turn them into learning moments, as I stated earlier in this chapter. When our kids fight, as siblings do—and trust me, I wondered if it would *ever* end when my kids' fighting looked like it would cause bodily harm to one another—take the opportunity to teach them

- Reflective listening, by actively listening to the words and feeling of the other then paraphrase back to let them know they are being heard and understood.

- Hearing and trying to understand another person's point of view

- Communicating their desires in a clear, respectful manner

- Sacrifice

- Negotiation

- Forgiveness

Overall, we want them to be able to handle conflict without parental supervision or intervention, as the case may sometimes be. Through this, we teach our children not just to survive, but to thrive. Not only can we develop their brains, but we can nurture and nourish their relational skills and their character. Of course, once they begin to thrive, we can rest assured when they come into more complex situations in their teens and early adulthood, they will be well equipped.

Build the Foundation

We know that in order to parent using Danish techniques, we need to understand our child. It sounds complicated, but it really isn't. We love our children and we want only the best for them. So let's learn about them. Once we do, there should be fewer stressful situations and we can all move forward on the journey with as few detours as possible.

Think of it like cooking a meal. If you don't understand how long it takes to cook one component, such as potatoes, how will you know when to start the other parts of the meal? If you understand how something works, it becomes easier to put a plan into motion.

It was a bit of an adjustment when I made dinner on my own for the first time. My mom had told me to figure out the menu ahead of time. But she also warned me that I needed to know how long each part of dinner would take to cook because I didn't want my entrée to get cold while waiting for the side dish to cook. Of course, I also didn't want my side to get cold while the entrée was prepared. It comes naturally to me now, but it was a learning curve at first.

Parenting our kids is like that. We have these amazing little people in our lives, and we want what's best for them. We think we understand that everyone is unique and we all react differently to influences and surroundings. We follow a parenting book that tells us what to do for each age until we realize what the book's "experts" say is not happening with our kids, or maybe it is but at a different age or another level.

The answer is to figure out how *your* child works and gain some insight into their behavior. Some of this is generalized, which includes understanding the brain's functions, but it is also specialized because once you observe your child's response to something that has happened, you can better understand how to help them adjust that response for their health and well-being. This will help make the parenting journey a little smoother and less full of potholes.

The Science Behind the Brain

Now we will lay out the scientific explanation behind a child's brain and why the Danish parenting style works so well in correlation with how children learn and grow. I was especially interested in this portion of parenting, because I studied early childhood education at university and I am fascinated by child development. The correlation between the brain and external influences was a topic I always wanted to fully understand. Therefore, I've embraced the part of parenting that allows me to use my education.

For starters, every one of us has felt like it's just too much, it's too hard, the kids aren't willing to listen, and most of all we can't live up to the image we have of the super-parent who never seems to struggle. There is always that one parent posting images of the wonderful meal she's prepared after working all day, picking up the kids from school, and then doing household chores while helping with homework. Yes, we all know at least one.

But let's be real. That super-parent doesn't exist. So that mom had one good day out of how many? And even if every day for her is perfect, well, she's missing out on some of the more "real" parts of life: the challenge, the adventure, or the thrill of seeing who will win when it comes to dinner consumption and bedtime. The bottom line is that no parent is perfect, and no child is perfect. As parents, we need to learn how to use the bad times as teaching tools.

Understanding our children's brains will help us know what to do during those teaching moments. Another note for this chapter—children are capable of understanding information about how their brain works, and when we share the information with them, they can begin to better understand their emotions and thoughts. This will enable them to figure out how to handle intense or difficult situations because they have a deeper insight into why they feel the way they do.

Parts of the Brain

Like the rest of the body, our brain is made up of parts. Think of the parts of the brain acting like our heart, veins, nerves, and so on in the body. Without one, the others cannot properly function. For example, so that the heart can beat, blood must be pumped through the veins. Similarly, each part of the brain has a separate function, and they all control a different portion of how we make decisions and view life.

Some parts of the brain are rational, while others are irrational. Some are reflective, while others are reactive. I know most of us have heard of the parts of the brain, and the terms "left brain" or "right brain" get thrown around in conversation when we talk about ourselves. But, as parents, we need to have a deeper understanding of those parts of the brain. We want our children to become well-balanced individuals able to navigate life with the best tools possible, so let's figure out how their brain works to equip them with what they need.

I'd like to share some information from Medical News Today about the brain and its processes (Rush & Burgess, 2023).

Left Brain

The left side, or hemisphere, of the brain controls speech and abstract thinking. It is the analytical, logical, detail-oriented side of the brain that is dominant in speech production.

Right Brain

The right side of the brain controls image processing and spatial thinking. It is the creative, free-thinking, intuitive side, and it's dominant in emotions.

In their book *The Whole-Brain Child*, Siegel and Bryson (2011)—a neuropsychiatrist and a parenting expert—explain the upstairs and downstairs brain. This is a concept that's meant to be shared with both adults and children alike. The upstairs brain and downstairs brain differ in a few key ways.

Upstairs Brain

The upstairs brain has more intricate brain processes, such as planning, decision-making, self-awareness, morality, and empathy. When the upstairs brain is working, the child or individual can slow down to think before they act or speak, regulate their emotions, self-soothe, and take into account the feelings of others. This part of the brain is not finished developing until we are in our twenties, so in children, it's a work in progress.

Downstairs Brain

The downstairs brain is where basic functions like breathing and blinking take place. Emotions and impulses, such as anger or fear, are also controlled by the downstairs brain. The downstairs brain is ruled by instinct and it's fully functioning from the time we're children, as it's completely developed at a young age.

Integration

Integration refers to the brain working as a team. It is the act of taking both the upstairs and downstairs parts and the right and left sides and helping them to work together as a whole.

When children's brains are not integrated, meltdowns and tantrums take place. Kids become easily overwhelmed by experiences, and they can't figure out how to handle their own emotions—let alone understand the emotions of others. This is a loss of integration or dis-integration. Because integration is the process of the brain working together as a coordinated and balanced whole, losing that balance between the regions of the brain makes the brain less able to work together as a healthy, complete part of the body. When we talk about integrating the brain, we mean the following:

- **Horizontally integrated:** The logic of the left brain can work in tandem with the emotion of the right brain.

- **Vertically integrated:** The thoughtful upstairs brain and the instinctual downstairs brain work together.

The authors of *The Whole Brain Child* point out that parents should not expect their children to make good decisions and think of others all the time. It is not going to happen, and it's expecting too much of your child. This sets your child up for failure, which isn't fair to them or to you. Because their upstairs brain is still incomplete, they will not be able to access all that they need to be the fully integrated individual that you're looking for. They need time, and their brain still has a lot to learn (Siegel & Bryson, 2011).

It's also important to note that strong emotions like fear, anger, trauma, and danger can overwhelm the upstairs brain. At these times, your child will be unable to access the upstairs brain, and it's a good idea for parents to recognize the symptoms. When the blocked access happens, create emotional and physical contact with your child. Hugs, love, and distraction are ways to help the child regain their mental balance and perspective. Once they've gotten their strong emotions under control, they can begin to access the upstairs brain functions.

It can be difficult to deal with our children when their emotions are so big and overwhelming. My husband and I might be adults with a fully functioning upstairs brain, but sometimes it's still a bit much. It has taken practice for us to work with the children when this overload of emotions happens.

We usually can use the "disagreeing appropriately" technique as we discussed in chapter one, where we are patient and listen to what upset them and why they were unhappy with a decision we'd made in those times when they needed to be heard. But sometimes, our daughter simply had a meltdown because her emotions were too much and she couldn't function enough to let us know what she needed. For example, our daughter sometimes had meltdowns over something that would have been easily resolved if she could have calmed down to discuss it.

In those situations, we changed our approach. We recognized that continuing to talk about the situation would only make it worse because she was incapable, at that moment, of being calm. Instead, she was in the fight-or-flight mode and trapped in the downstairs brain. My husband handled this time best because he was able to look at what was missing and why she was trapped, thus helping her find a way through her emotions. For example if she is whiny and has been on the couch for too long she may want a snack or physical movement. If she gets her feelings hurt while playing a game outside, maybe she needs water and a joke or story. He was able to keep her mind off the problem until she had calmed down enough to address the situation and let her voice be heard in a calm manner.

How Integration Takes Place

Everything around us, no matter our age, has a profound effect on our brain. Your brain is like an electrical component of your body. Neurons get fired up every time they're used, and over time they form a bridge of sorts that connects one part of the brain to another. It is amazing how the brain works and that it has the ability to be reshaped or re-formed. This process is called neural plasticity. It has been found that regular habits form and strengthen these bridges. This is why it takes time to build habits and sometimes even more to break them. You are not just breaking an undesirable habit you literally have to allow your brain to heal from it!

For children, especially, that reshaping is happening constantly. Their neural pathways and bridges are being built and deepened with each choice and inter-action. Their experiences and reactions are helping them develop and see what makes them unique and brings them happiness. They're like a huge canvas just waiting for a masterpiece to be unfolded. Honestly, everything we do and all the stuff we go through affects the wiring in our brain. This is why it is so important to give our children as many experiences as possible. They will connect the different parts of the brain naturally, and that experience will give them more data from which they can better understand the world and determine their part in it.

When the parts of the brain work together regularly, they begin to work on a higher level. That means, for example, it becomes normal for the left and right brain to work together. The brain accomplishes more because it's able to use its full capacity.

The Danish parenting style allows parents to work with their children to get their brains integrated. Here are some ways to help your children begin integrating the various parts of their brain:

- When your child is experiencing strong emotions and is unable to connect with their upstairs brain, get them moving. Exercise or some energetic play is best at this point. Once they've worked out the excess emotion, play a game called "What would you do if..." or another game that involves questions designed to access the upstairs brain.

- There's another game to teach your kids when they're young and struggling with out-of-control emotions. It's called "Name it to tame it," and the idea of this game is for children to name the feelings they're experiencing. This game helps release chemicals that children need to calm down and regain emotional control so they can use their upstairs brain.

- Talk with your children about their experiences, even when the event was a negative one. Going over the facts of what happened will bring in the logical left side of the brain. This gets the right and left brain working together and gives the child the necessary components to balance the emotional side of the situation with the factual side. When you do this, you give your child a more efficient way to access the memories and emotions they experienced, allowing them the chance to recognize and understand them for future reference. By giving words (using the left brain) to your feelings (your right brain), the child is integrating both sides of the brain. It also makes the feeling less scary or intimidating because the child understands what they were feeling and how it came about.

- If your child is shy, give them opportunities to explore. Provide them with a sense of courage that will help diminish their inhibitions. A word of caution, though—if your child feels that they are being overly protected or thrown into stressful situations with no backup, their shyness will become more pronounced.

Since this is such a big topic I was only able to give an overview of how the brain works. If you would like more detail please see the references. Clearly we want the best for our children, and we will be able to provide that when we have a better understanding of what is happening in their brain. We need to know how to approach life situations in a way that will enable them to live a happier, healthier, more effective life.

We also want them to feel complete, and I think that will come about when we understand how to get their whole brain working together with all the parts of the brain showcasing the meaning of teamwork.

The beauty of it is that we don't need to be a neuroscientist to understand our child's brain. We have books like *The Whole Brain Child,* written by experts in their field, to help us understand what our children need. What I find really exciting is that all of the information in this book connects with the Danish parenting style in many ways. Part of parenting is understanding our child's type, which correlates with an understanding of how a child's brain works. It's nice to know that this parenting adventure we're on while stems from the heart and home of Nordic living, is backed by science.

Mental Health for the Whole Family

In today's world, the mental health crisis is continuing to escalate, and its effects can be seen across every generation, but especially in the new adults trying to find their place in this complex world. The magic of parenting in the Danish way is not just for parenting, but it is an invitation to a lifestyle that takes a holistic approach. Yes, we are focused on raising children to be strong, kind and empathetic adults. Part of that is learning to become strong, kind and empathetic adults ourselves. As we hone our skills, heal from our childhoods and practice what we learn, we will have better mental health and be more capable of providing a firm foundation for our children. They can in turn be the kind of parents we would hope to be.

Raise Children to Be Adults

This topic can arouse controversy, since many people feel that it is another way of pushing children to grow up too fast. But let's look at it from another perspective: from the lens of the Danish family. Especially in today's world, our children are going to be exposed to more adult experiences than we might like, and often we have little to no control over what they're seeing or hearing. As parents, the one thing we can control is how our children respond to this exposure.

I want to reframe how we view the wording in the subheading above, "Raise Children to be Adults." I think many people interpret that as treating them like small adults, giving them free rein to make all their own choices, and including them in adult decisions. That is not what the Danish parenting style promotes. By raising our children to be adults, we are simply giving them the tools to become successful grown-ups, understand how to make their own decisions, and ultimately trust their decision-making process. If we spend their childhood shielding our kids from everything—making their choices and decisions for them—they are going to struggle when they grow up and suddenly have to make choices for themselves.

Ultimately, we want our children to have critical thinking skills and clear decision-making tools to navigate the dark paths and more sinister trails of life. Whether we like it or not, our children are going to stumble upon narrow, twisty paths filled with the pitfalls of poor decision-making, so why not give them what they need to avoid the traps?

For example, 46% of parents today believe that children under age 11 are exposed to age-inappropriate material through video content during screen time on their phones, laptops, or tablets (Auxier et al., 2020). Of course, too much use of electronic devices can negatively affect a child's ability to self-regulate, which does not lead to good decision-making. The moment children pick up a smartphone or log into their tablet, they could be plunged into the adult world with no parental guidance. It does not even have to be our children with this access, it may be from those they come in contact with.

The bottom line for all this talk about screen time and our children is that the Danish style of parenting begins to teach children the skills they need to make good decisions early in life. They start to learn the consequences of not just their actions, but their decisions, at a young age.

The use of electronic devices is inevitable and a huge part of our society today. Therefore, our children are going to be faced with grown-up decisions sooner than parents would like. They should have appropriate tools to make those decisions from a more adult perspective no matter the age. Remember, "Train up a child in the way he should go: and when he is old, he will not depart from it" (*King James Bible*, 2024/1769, Proverbs 22:6).

We must remember that our children learn by observation and experience. They observe our behavior and copy it, but they also figure it out by making their own decisions and then gaining insight from the outcome of their choices. Yes, this is an adult concept, but we can't expect them to navigate the world of adulthood the moment they come of age. They must be prepared for it.

Their childhood will stay intact; they will be learning throughout their younger years that their parents are there for them, we support them, and we have their best interests at heart. But they will also know that we trust them enough to figure out how to navigate their life with the skills we've given them. We all want to have a say in what we do in our lives, and that is one of the most important things we can teach our kids.

The benefit of allowing our children to make decisions for themselves is that they begin with small decisions that can be worked through if things don't go as hoped. As we get older, the stakes get higher, and I would rather have my children learn how to handle choices and the results when they are young and the backlash from a poor decision isn't as painful or difficult.

Let Them Keep Their Autonomy

I discussed how children gain autonomy through play in Chapter 4, and that concept is important for raising them to be adults as well. To put it simply, autonomy is the ability to control one's own life. We want to raise children to understand the process that is involved in having the self-assurance to make those vital decisions.

I believe it is so important to start, right from the beginning, to teach children that they are the architects of their lives. It is up to them to decide what they want to be, how they want to act, and, really, how they're going to interact with the rest of the world. No matter how many times they struggle or how many times they face what seems to be insurmountable odds, they are always in control. I can't tell you how many times, as a parent, I just wanted to take control back or make all their decisions for them, because seeing them struggle can be the most painful part of parenting.

It gets easier. Remember, the upstairs brain isn't fully developed in children until their twenties, so little side paths or forks in the road are going to be encountered. What I finally drilled into my head was that all the potholes and the debris that we trip over along the way are all life lessons. By successfully navigating these stumbling blocks, we are growing stronger. So no matter how often my children struggle, I know they'll make it and they're building the resilience they need to stand up against what life gives us.

So I guess what I'm trying to say is that by letting my kids learn for themselves and giving them the ability to discover their autonomy, I'm giving them what they need to be stronger adults who can face the difficulties that stand before them and persevere. As our children learn the decision making process and understand how to handle the consequences of their decisions they will fortify their mental health. They will be well practiced in decision making from their youth, and therefore have a sense of self confidence and be empowered to make clear decisions which will reduce anxiety and increase probability of success in whatever they chose to do in life.

Everyone Has the Right to Be Heard

Very often in families, the child who is most vocal gets the most attention. Danish families teach their children that everyone has a right to be heard, not just the one who does the most complaining or crying.

I knew a family with three kids: a girl and two boys. The middle boy was the toughest one, with a solid build. He played sports and was sure of himself. The youngest boy was a bit of a scrawny child, all arms and legs, and it took him a while to grow into those long limbs. The youngest would nag at the middle boy, doing things that would frustrate his brother until the older brother would retaliate. Because of his size and abilities, he could make that retaliation hurt. The youngest would then go crying to his parents about how mean his brother was and how he had hurt him. The middle boy tried to defend himself and his parents usually would automatically take the side of the younger, scrawny boy. They assumed that because he was so much smaller, his older brother had been picking on him.

In the Danish method of parenting, though, parents recognize that it is important to hear both sides of the story before assuming anything. Just because someone is smaller than another person does not mean they are innocent of all wrongdoing. Parents know that they can teach empathy to their children by caring enough to hear each side of the story.

Social Skills

The Danish parenting style does not judge a child for saying "No" and wanting to play with their toy alone without sharing or even trading. When children learn that nobody is going to force them to do something they don't want to, they are more authentic with themselves. They learn that they can be honest. Too often, we try to teach our children to do something just to make someone else happy. Yes, empathy means that we care about others, but it does not mean that we must do what others want just to make them happy while sacrificing our own wants.

Danish parents also make sure to point out the emotions of others, and then ask their child why the other person might be experiencing that emotion. They get on the same eye level as the child while talking to them, showing that they're acknowledging the child and their feelings. Parents make sure to show that there is no judgment, which teaches the child respect.

Danish families also read and tell a lot of stories to their children, especially books that increase empathy, because they address all emotions and deal with life in a very real way.

Empathy and Kindness

We would like to think that children are naturally empathetic, and they do learn early to recognize emotions in others. However, empathy is not a trait someone does or does not have. Empathy is something we must learn, and in Danish families, it is taught both in school and at home. It's not necessarily that Danish parents specifically say to their children that it's time to learn empathy. Their kids are learning how to be empathetic, along with the kindness that goes hand-in-hand with that trait, through the everyday lessons their parents are demonstrating and teaching.

Danish children are taught empathy within their schools as well. In fact, they're not taught to judge the feelings of others but simply to recognize what those feelings are. Children are grouped together and each group has children with varying strengths and weaknesses. Within these groups, the children learn how to help each other while recognizing the positive qualities of others.

They are shown pictures of kids demonstrating various emotions, and then they talk about these emotions. The children are encouraged to put into words what the pictures show. This teaches children to understand feelings, not just in themselves but in others.

It's important to know that Danish families embrace the idea that happiness comes to us when we have "interaction and support of others" (Alexander & Andersson, 2022). Empathy is what connects us to people, making it one of the most important qualities we can teach our children. These connections of feeling loved, cared for and valued are important to our mental and physical health.

Walsh and Walsh (2019), writing for *Psychology Today,* tell us what to look for in children when it comes to empathy. How we are all born with the ability to show empathy, but it doesn't just happen. It is a work in progress that starts with the parents and takes experience and practice. But at the end of the journey, there are specific things children will do to show that they understand empathy and practice it:

1. Recognize that they are individuals, with feelings and perspectives that are different from others.

2. Name their feelings and know that others have the same feelings.

3. Regulate their emotional responses.

4. Understand how another person feels.

5. Think about what would make another person feel better.

Parents Shouldn't Hide Their Feelings

Children get confused if their parents hide their emotional reactions, which sometimes happens when an adult feels that they need to protect their children. For example, when a loved one dies, the parents might be worried that grief will overwhelm their children so they hide their own sadness. Often, a parent will worry that they won't be able to guide their child through the grieving process if they are too caught up in their own sorrow. But this does not help the child learn how to

1. Express their grief

2. Understand the grieving process in others

3. Recognize grief and sadness and what it looks like in others

Everyone expresses grief in their own way, just like we all show joy in different ways. Let me give you an example of how, as a parent, you can recognize how your children show grief in their own unique way and support them accordingly.

A friend had two daughters. The oldest was very reserved while her younger sister was emotional, wearing her heart on her sleeve. Each of the girls expressed joy and grief in different ways, but they also understood how the other sister showed their emotions and learned to be empathetic to others because of this.

For example, tears came quickly to the youngest girl, whether they were tears of joy or sadness. She was bouncy and sometimes a little giddy when happiness was the emotion of the day. The oldest daughter, though, internalized everything and while she experienced the same pain or excitement, she was not the kind to express those emotions for everyone to see.

In this case, their mother saw the need early on to help her girls learn how to "read" others. She had the perfect teaching tool for her daughters' personality differences, and it helped the girls understand how to recognize and care about others' feelings. They learned how to respect people's feelings, even when the expressions of those emotions did not match how each girl personally manifested them.

Develop a Resilient Emotional Foundation

Danish parenting techniques focus on what is truly important so parents can give children what they need to emotionally and mentally guide children through their lives. You will find that Danish parents place a higher significance on a sense of togetherness while fostering minimalism.

Minimalism in Danish culture is part of hygge, making it an essential part of their lifestyle. It "embraces simplicity, functionality, and a connection to the natural world" (Erickson, 2023), which makes sense when you think about it. I've told you about how hygge is the backbone of Danish society and culture, and it's such an integral way of life for them that it makes sense to bring that sense of calm into their homes.

To foster hygge and the sense of togetherness that it brings about, Danish parents don't need to fill their homes with stuff. Their kids don't need more toys than one room will hold, and Danish families don't want to spend time moving decorative pillows, blankets, or stuffies off a couch for visitors to relax with a cup of coffee by the fire.

Danes like homes that radiate tranquility and peace and don't overwhelm your senses the moment you walk in the door. They don't believe that this is the way to experience true hygge, and they're correct. I can't even count how many times I've been distracted when I'm in a room filled with clutter, or just filled with stuff on every wall and in every corner. It always makes me feel as though the room is closing in on me and I'll be swallowed up by someone's thimble collection, or their porcelain doll collection will bury me in frilly dresses and ringlet-curled hair.

Children are easily distracted; I think we all know this to be true. Put them in a room full of brightly colored trinkets and they will lose sight of what they're doing like children following the Pied Piper, being led to an uncertain demise by the shininess and sheer volume of what is surrounding them.

So when you put a child into a room that is filled with only what is necessary, making it calm and soothing, their brain will be better able to concentrate. They can focus, and not just on their studies. We must be able to focus when we read a book, put a puzzle together, or just have a conversation with someone. Nothing is worse than talking to someone who is constantly distracted.

I'm not here to tell you to run out and begin decluttering or to get rid of everything you own. We don't have to do that, because the minimalist way of Danish culture is to keep what is important. And really, if you're not a fan of minimalism, there's nothing to say you can't create a room specifically for your child where they can focus on whatever task they are working on. I find that I need to focus even to watch television, since I'm easily distracted.

The bottom line is that children need a clutter-free environment to focus on what is important. They need to cultivate a sense of calm and mental clarity. This supports their cognitive development so they can move through the world with confidence. When we value experiences over possessions, we are better able to thrive creatively. This calm, relaxing environment will also nurture a deeper connection with the family.

Danish parenting teaches us that life is about savoring the little moments, discovering joy in shared activities, and creating a foundation of emotional richness that will be with us forever.

Turn "Me" Into "We"

Danish culture emphasizes "social connectedness rather than division" (Alexander & Andersson, 2022). They do this by focusing on something called *fællesskab*, which translates to community or togetherness. It's that sense we get when we feel a part of something and belong to a special group that holds meaning for us.

When you're a part of something so deeply felt that holds such value, you gain a deeper sense of happiness. It just feels right to be part of something so important. Therefore, this *fællesskab* is like hygge; it's a vital part of Danish culture and their education system.

Fællesskab is what leads to *trivsel*, which is the Danish way of saying that they are thriving or that their well-being is high. When families experience a strong sense of togetherness, their *trivsel* is high, which is good. It means they feel seen and heard, like someone is there for them when they're sad or upset, and they are able to help someone else who is sad or upset.

For our children, when the quality of *fællsskab* is high—meaning when they experience togetherness—it will positively impact every part of their life. This includes "improved learning, better involvement, higher competence levels, and an increased peace of mind" (Alexander & Andersson, 2022).

But there are two ways that *fællsskab* can become a part of life. One is the kind that comes from hygge, and it happens when we experience a sense of togetherness when we play games together or just interact with people we love. The other kind is when we feel a sense of belonging to a group that we didn't want to be a part of at first.

That doesn't mean you join some weird group or anything like that. It comes from collaborating with someone that you wouldn't necessarily choose to work with. Maybe your child is on the playground and there's a kid that nobody really likes because they're a bully or they're so shy. But this second kind of *fællsskab* is when our children learn the value of "we" over "me." They learn to give up a small piece of themselves for the whole.

It can mean embracing the idea that you have to give something to get something. For example, your child is playing with a group of kids and things are not going as they had planned. The project they're working on is not working out, and your child's ideas aren't cutting it. In comes compromise—something we all need to learn, of course. Your child grudgingly sees the wisdom of accepting someone else's idea, so they accept the compromise. All the ideas blend into the perfect project and suddenly, even though they had to give in on one idea, your child belongs to this group of kids who accomplished an exciting task.

I have simplified this idea, but I've shared several resources at the end of this book and encourage you to explore further if you want to get a full sense of how *fællsskab* works and how it can impact your family's life.

Habits to Increase Mental Health and Well-Being

I have compiled a list of things I do—habits I've developed—that help me stay happy. No matter what we, as parents, do for and with our children, we face burnout and parental stress. As we all know, there is a lot of pressure to be the "perfect" parent, and even knowing we shouldn't allow that pressure to creep in does not alleviate the stress that comes with it. Here are the habits I've created that I hope will help you travel this parenting journey with grace:

1. Take time to rest and relax several times a day. Put away technology and ignore your cell phone while you take the time to sit back and relax with a cup of tea or hot chocolate.

2. Perform simple meditations during the day. They don't have to be complicated, and I focus on them once in the morning and once at night. If you need or want to meditate in the middle of the day, go for it—even if all you do is sit for 10 minutes and take some deep breaths.

3. Live as much as possible right now. Take the time to enjoy the view wherever you go—there is always something beautiful around us. Try to live in the moment, not the past or the future. I have discovered, through personal experience, that extensively dwelling on what was or what could be isn't healthy.

4. Open-air living is key. Embrace *friluftsliv*. Take a walk in the park, or find a peaceful, green environment at lunchtime. You will be amazed at how these little things restore your energy and help you feel more

relaxed. Outside time is important and is the heart of *friluftsliv* and *kos*. That's a new word, I know, and it refers to the kind of immediate happiness you experience when you're safe, warm, and happy.

5. Serve others. I enjoy helping my neighbors and friends, even with small things. I don't have to do something show-stopping or dramatic; it can be a simple act of kindness such as helping them carry groceries into their house or even picking up a gallon of milk for them when I'm at the store.

6. Have meaningful conversations. I love sharing what I've learned with others and I genuinely enjoy hearing from others about what they're learning. There is so much development and growth from learning, and it's a joy to share with others.

7. Carve out time for date nights. I look forward to the occasional date night when my husband and I can just spend time together. Sometimes we explore new places together, or we find new buildings so we can explore their architecture and history as a couple. It was exciting, also, knowing that I could share my newfound knowledge with the kids during homeschooling.

8. Say some gratitude prayers. I spend time each day recounting the things I'm grateful for. This makes me happy, because all that gratitude makes me realize how fortunate we are and how happy our family is.

The above list is just my way of sharing with you how I experience *kos*, the things that make me happier and healthier. Remember, we're going to feel less stress and believe we're doing a better job when we take the time to embrace our own mental well-being, not just that of our kids. For children to be happy, parents need to be happy.

To wrap things up, parents can experience "mom guilt," the inescapable feeling we get when we do our best for our children and give them everything they need but then they wander off the path. Something happens and suddenly everything we did for them—teaching them to effectively self-govern, teaching them about health, explaining good communication with a full grasp of consequences, and promoting responsible decision-making—seems like an absolute failure. We start second-guessing ourselves.

But take a step back and realize that mistakes are going to be made, and once you understand how a child's brain works, it will hopefully lessen that guilt. And remember, everything is a process, so what you are teaching your children, everything they are experiencing, and all the life lessons they are figuring out will take time.

In addition, keep in mind that nothing and nobody is perfect. If you're trying this parenting style for the first time, you need to remember that it is not something you're familiar with. You're coming from a completely different culture—a different way of thinking, really. And you're unlearning everything you know and replacing it with a method that is foreign to you.

However, you're here because you feel deeply that there is a better way to raise your children. The typical parent mindset is that we want our children to have more or better than we did, and that goes for life experiences. We want our children to be happier, healthier, smarter—whatever the "more" is, we want it for them. So you're looking at a parenting journey that you hope leads them to being a member of the happiest people in the world.

Living the Danish Way of Parenting

This last chapter is the final stage of all the other chapters, with a practical approach for how to put this parenting style into effect. Now that you've read the other chapters, you're probably wondering how you're supposed to get it done; this is the chapter that will help you with that process.

Is Danish Parenting for You?

Parenting is a unique journey, which might be a surprise to some. It may seem like all parents are following the same path, but even if we use the same parenting strategy, we follow that road in our own way. The journey is influenced by the values, goals, and dreams we have for our family.

Of course, there are days when it is easy to forget that it is not about surviving the chaos; it is about nurturing the future. With this in mind, there are some questions that you can ask yourself before deciding if Danish parenting is the right path for you and your family. Keep in mind that although this book is about Danish parenting techniques, I have tried to show you that there are ways to supplement this style with other practices.

Once you decide you want to follow Danish parenting practices, pick and choose what it is you want for your family. Take the pieces of this parenting style and apply them to your family life. Ultimately, it is up to you to decide what you're looking for. It has to feel right for your family.

I've got a list of questions, or a quiz of sorts, to help you determine if the Danish parenting style is for you. Rate each question, with 1 meaning you don't do it at all and 10 meaning you parent that way already. Here we go:

1. How often do you listen to your child share their concerns and feelings all the way through, without thinking about what you want to say before they're done speaking?

2. In the last week, have you given your child a genuine "I am sorry" about the way you reacted or behaved, with no "buts" after the apology?

3. In the last week, have you been open-minded to new parenting techniques and those new approaches to parenting?

4. Have you stayed consistent in your expectations of your child?

5. Do you stay consistent with how you respond to your child's behavior?

6. Have you played or talked about something your child is interested in?

7. Have you had some one-on-one time in nature with your child?

8. Have you rewarded your child's good behavior more than punishing the bad behavior (through verbal praise reward systems and tangible rewards)?

9. Have you noticed any changes in your child's life that may be leading to their behavioral changes, and if so did you give them grace?

10. Have you spent time reading to your children, in family reading sessions when they're young or a family book club setting when they're older, followed by an open discussion about what was read?

These questions are not to make you feel as though you cannot take this parenting journey; they are simply to help you evaluate where you are and where you want to go. They might open up areas that you had not thought of when it comes to parenting and might even help you come to the conclusion that the Danish way of parenting is for you.

How to Start This Parenting Style

Once you've established the Danish parenting style within your household, there are many things you can do. It's a good reminder that this parenting style is a balance between discipline, emotional awareness, and independence. It's important to start slowly and to incorporate the portions of this parenting style that are the most important to you. For instance, maybe you want to start with hygge, so you'll begin creating cozy corners to incorporate quality bonding time within the family. Maybe you want to start including your kids in some of your decision-making. Remember, it is most likely a new way of life for your family, and it's going to take some adjusting. But if you follow the guidelines I've listed here, it should help ease everyone into the new way of doing things.

In Setting Rules

Remember that most rules are determined by the whole family in those family discussions we talked of in Chapter 2, Exploring Danish Parenting. When communicating these rules together the goal is to allow all to have a voice as well as all know and agree to the guidelines, boundaries, and expectations you have for family behavior.

Establish Consequences

Once you've set the consequences, you must follow through when appropriate.

Be Compassionate

It's vital to be warm, empathetic, and supportive of your child.

Focus on a Strong, Supportive Relationship

Don't try to control everything they do; instead show them that you love and support their decision-making. Rather than question their choices, talk about them, offer encouragement for a well-planned decision, and offer helpful guidance in a positive manner.

Encourage Independence

Children must understand the natural consequences of their actions, which means they must experience both the good and the bad. You are there as a loving support system, but they will have to understand the consequences of their actions.

Find Balance

It probably doesn't feel right at first, but start by letting your child make more decisions. Have regular, open discussions about their choices. The happy medium you need might seem elusive at first, but it will start to feel more natural over time.

Your version of the Danish parenting style might be a mix of various styles and look a little different from how anyone else in your family parents. That is okay, though, and once you've worked on it for a while, you will find the perfect blend that fits your family.

Before I forget, there may be parts of Danish parenting that don't resonate with your family, especially at first. I know you might want to jump right into creating those "perfect" family moments that bring a sense of togetherness and strengthen the bond you all share. However, it might take a bit for everyone, yourself included, to get on board with hygge, for example. Definitely don't force it, because you lose the feeling of togetherness when your kids or spouse feel like you're making them do something they aren't interested in.

Start small and let it happen naturally. When we started the family dinner and family game night, our kids struggled at first. It took a little time before they finally began viewing it as something they wanted to do, not something they were forced to do. We had to "go with the flow," for example. If something truly important was happening for one of us, as parents we had to be willing to move the family dinner night or postpone it. Once our children realized that we weren't going to cancel an event of theirs that they had been looking forward to, they also realized that we had their best interests at heart. Family dinner and game night finally started to become something they actively looked forward to each week.

Experiences

When I'm learning something new, I always feel like real-life examples help me understand a process. I've put together some of what stands out to me that I hope will help you understand Danish parenting techniques and how we've worked them into our family life:

- My son has told us that he liked the Disagreeing Appropriately portion of parenting. I think it was tough for the kids at first, because they thought it would be a constant round of getting their way because they presented their argument for what they wanted. But my husband and I explained there are going to be times we would have to say "no" and we needed them to respect that. We let them know that we would prefer to say "yes," but sometimes it just wasn't possible. The beauty of this part of our parenting technique was that we all had the ability to state what was said, express what we wanted, and explain how the problem was solved. A lot of tantrums were avoided this way and there were fewer arguments. My kids soon left behind the days of whining because they didn't get what they asked for.

- Our family has had many opportunities to use the "ABC method," as I call it, to say we're sorry:

  - **A:** Admit what we did wrong.

  - **B:** Be sorry; acknowledge how what we did affected the other person, then say we are sorry.

  - **C:** Correct it by asking if there's a way to help, or just fix it.

Once, my daughter was building a block castle but my son knocked it down. When he used the ABC method, my daughter felt heard and validated, while my son recognized what he did and how it made her feel and corrected what he had done by rebuilding it.

- When my daughter was 4, there was a sweet moment between us when I realized she had learned empathy and was trying to show respect. We had a field day with some other families and my daughter asked me to push her on the swings. After some time of me pushing her she said, "Mom, you don't have to push me anymore. You can go and do what you want." I was touched because I realized that at such a young age, she was empathetic to my wants and wanted me to be happy, as well.

- We taught our children to listen to their conscience: to be aware and listen to what it's telling them. This helped them build their identity of who they are as a person when they listened to what was right or wrong.

- It was a learning process for me, as well as the kids, because I knew I was setting the example. So I had to follow through with what I was telling them they should do by doing it myself. For example, I often told the kids to wear a jacket outside so they would stay warm. Therefore, even if I didn't feel like putting on my coat, I did so because I was setting an example for them. I know they needed to learn the natural consequences of any action but I also learned that they needed to see the good consequences, not just the negative.

- We played a family game that we called, "unfortunately, but fortunately." This game teaches children to see the good in any situation. Each person contributes the next line to the story that unfolds, but the trick is that it has to start with "fortunately" or "unfortunately." Here is an example:

"A man was walking through the woods. Unfortunately, he was lost."

"Fortunately, he came upon a signpost that pointed the way back to town."

"Unfortunately, it also said the town was 5 miles away."

"Fortunately, the path had many beautiful things to see."

"Unfortunately, he was tired and hungry."

"Fortunately, after only walking for a couple of minutes, he heard a car drive up behind him."

"Unfortunately, it was a very small car and it looked like every seat was filled, so it didn't look like there would be room for the man."

"Fortunately, when the car stopped, one person got out and waved goodbye, since they had reached their destination."

"Unfortunately, when the man asked for a ride, he found out that the car and its occupants were turning around and going back the other way."

"Fortunately, the person who had gotten out of the car heard the conversation and told the man there was a motel and diner just around the bend."

Our children reminded themselves through the stories that while something unfortunate may happen, there were things that could turn it into something fortunate. Our family went to a museum once and it wasn't the trip we thought it would be. Traffic was awful, and then one exhibit that we really wanted to see was closed. But afterward, we were able to talk to the kids and let them see that their parents also had the unfortunate experience but we were able to talk about the trip and see the fortunate things that came from it. So many disappointing things happened, but there were fortunate things that came out of it, too.

- My daughter as a toddler loved when we role-played with her. She called it "acting back" when she would be the director and us the actors.

Basically, she liked it when we joined in her pretend play or make-believe fun. She used to invite us to her "beauty shop" where her magic unicorn helped her. We dressed up and tried on the accessories with her. Our son still loves telling us about the games he imagines, and he loves that we are interested in what he is doing. Our daughter also loved to color, and it was always more fun for her when we joined her and colored with her. She was even happy when we sat and listened to her while she colored. She loved to tell stories about what she was coloring or just what was on her mind.

Incorporating Danish Parenting Into Your Family: A Practical Approach

I'd like to lay out the basic ground rules that can apply to families as well as everyone in general. We have to change our mindset in order to apply Danish parenting techniques to our lifestyle.

Prioritize the People You Love

Family and friends need to come first. It's not that your job is unimportant because, let's face it, we need money to survive. But take the time to visit your loved ones. Shopping or movies or just about anything else will always be there, but nobody lives forever. So, at the risk of sounding depressing, visit and share the love while you still can.

Eat Together

Sharing meals and time together is healthy and makes you happier. It's as simple as that.

Ditch the Fairytale Endings

Life is not perfect, and it is nice to lose yourself in a good fairy tale or a story with a happily-ever-after ending. Danish culture however, recognizes that these perfect life endings aren't realistic, and they accept life for what it is. Once you do this, you can be a happier version of yourself because you don't have expectations that cannot be met.

Have you ever wondered why the old, original fairy tales have such dark endings? Those original stories don't have the same happy endings as the Disney-fied fairy tales we know and love in our culture today. Remember, quite a few of the more famous fairy-tale authors have their roots in Scandinavian culture, so it makes sense that Danish culture would keep them foremost in their practices even today.

Rather than believing in the perfect outcome, Danish culture knows that reality is rough. But they would rather face that reality and make their happiness instead of embracing the happily-ever-after that Hallmark and Disney would have us believe (Russell, 2016).

As a parent, this is one of the things my husband struggled with, but it wasn't because he firmly believed everything would always turn out for the best. He grew up on the old fairy tales with the endings that were a bit sinister, or at least dark. However, we wanted our kids to be happy, and I struggled with the idea that teaching them the more realistic parts of those stories was good for them.

But when I thought about it, I realized that by teaching my children that no ending is perfect and that sometimes things don't work out, I was helping them. I was teaching them that most of the time we have to fight through the bad and make our own happy ending. But we have to be willing to work through the difficulties that can and will arise before we can get there.

Try Plan B

So, it's the holidays and the whole family is together in the house: eating, playing games, and visiting. It's stuffy, the kids are restless, and some of the adults are, as well. What do you do? Go outside, of course. Fresh air is good for us, as our mothers have been saying for generations. Give all family members a specific job and take those games outside. The kids can run off their pent-up energy and the adults can stretch their legs. Time to embrace *friluftsliv*!

When I think about our family's parenting journey, I realize there is one thing that could be an obstacle for other families. That some families do not embrace the outdoor life that can be found in Danish culture, it can be more difficult to implement that portion into your parenting style.

With so many of us living in urban environments, parents question how they can incorporate more outdoor playtime into their children's lives. It is a valid and often concerning issue that we all face, and I'd like to give some practical approaches to it here. I mentioned the ways to bring *friluftsliv* into our lives in Chapter 3, and it encompassed the understanding that it's more work when living in an urban area, where there are fewer forests or outdoor areas to explore. The ideas I shared in that chapter are all valid, but I wanted to give a few more practical suggestions.

When you want your children to have the opportunity to play outdoors, hike, or just explore nature, sometimes you have to be vocal to the right people. You have to do your research, find administrators and city officials who can help you, and keep following up so that what you want remains top of mind for them.

But beyond that, there are things to do that can be done closer to home: in your own backyard or even in a city. Every city has a park of some kind—some green space—and many activities can be done there. For example

- Build sculptures from what you find in nature—a walk in your neighborhood or spending some time in the backyard will allow your child to discover leaves, twigs, rocks, grass, weeds, or whatever else they can find. Then have them build sculptures from these items. Have them look for patterns in each of the outdoor goodies they find. Or, let them play in some mud using old pans, utensils, and household tools. My daughter just loves this. When I was a girl I used to make mud pies. I would carefully and painstakingly shape my mud into a circle, then decorate it with leaves and twigs.

- Go for a bike ride or take a walk. If you're in a heavily populated area and you're not comfortable with your child doing this on their own, make it a family outing. Go for a bike ride together. Encourage your child to pay attention to their surroundings during the ride, and talk about what they see when you reach your destination. The local park can be the destination and once you arrive, talk about the journey and what they saw. This is the perfect opportunity to teach them new words to describe their observations. Make sure you encourage them to talk about what they smelled, heard, and possibly even felt so they can engage all their senses. For example, was it a misty kind of day and what did that mist feel like?

- Go outside for storytime. Yes, I'm the first to say that it's great to curl up in a chair and read a good book. Get some fresh air while you're doing it; take a hammock, or blanket and a couple of books outside to find a shady tree or a bit of sun as your backdrop. When your children are really little, find some books that match what the day looks like. For example, if you have a couple of trees nearby, have your child observe and maybe try to find pine cones or twigs or leaves while also learning about that part of nature.

- Make some outdoor play dates—our children love when their friends can come to play, but why stop at just playing in the house? And, why stop at the playdate being just for the children? Arrange to meet up with another family at the park, where the parents can get together while their children play. Maybe you could plan a picnic with another family. Set up a hike and include your child's friend along with their family. Whatever the kids would like to do outdoors, find a way to include the adults, as well.

- I love the idea of a nature scavenger hunt. If your child collects rocks, this is a great time to add to the collection. Or, you could make a list of various birds, trees, animals, rocks, and so forth that you want the kids to find on the scavenger hunt. Have them cross each one off the list as they find them.

- Just play ball. Letting kids play outside with a soccer ball, playing catch with a baseball, or shooting hoops with a basketball is a great way to keep them entertained outdoors. For really little kids, a game of hot potato with a beach ball can be fun.

- Set up spy missions! This activity gets the parents involved and can be a lot of fun for adults and children. Get together with another family and have one family leave a "trail" for the other to follow. For example, this trail can be along a sidewalk using sidewalk chalk to make arrows and letters that spell out a secret message. Along a forest trail, sticks and rocks can point the way or spell out the secret message.

Some of these activities, like the spy missions, keep more than a child's body active. They keep the brain engaged, and the fresh air should add an extra boost to their brain activity.

Homeschooling Is a Good Option

Within my culture, Danish education techniques are not found in most school classrooms, so I looked into homeschooling my kids. Of course, I did my research and discovered that the literacy rate in Denmark is 99% (*What Is the Education System Like in Denmark?*, n.d.), so their literacy is quite high. With that in mind, here are a few of the reasons I believe homeschooling works well with Danish parenting techniques:

- **Emphasis on social skills:** When they're still very young, ages 3–6, students at the preschool level start learning numbers and letters, but the focus is primarily on social skills. There is a lot of free play and outdoor education with a strong focus on nature being the teacher.

- **Avoids class rankings and no formal tests:** Children begin their practical education at age 6 and the schools do not put an emphasis on class rankings. There are no formal tests at this level of schooling, either, so classes are not graded (*What Is the Education System Like in Denmark?*, n.d.). The way we normally test students in the US is not a fundamental approach in Denmark. In 2010 the country instituted national testing, but Danish students have scored well on these and made a good showing (OECD, 2022).

- **Emphasis on problem-solving and group collaborations:** Rather than rote memorization so students can score well on tests, Danish schools focus on teaching students how to problem-solve and work collaboratively in groups.

One aspect of homeschooling really appealed to me over the rest: the idea that I didn't have to consider my children to be in a certain grade, because they were just learning at whatever level they were at. I liked this freedom because I realized that my children are different and could be at one level for one subject but another level for another subject. For instance, one of my kids was great at math but did not enjoy reading. So he was frequently at a higher grade level for math than reading or even spelling. I could easily accommodate this difference within the homeschool structure.

I also liked the idea that, at least when the kids were young, math could be taught in the kitchen, the shop, or at a sewing machine. Math is all around us, and I loved it when my kids saw the opportunity to further their math skills when we were cooking dinner and needed to double or halve a recipe.

Another aspect of homeschooling that I really liked was that my kids could learn science by spending time outside in nature. Gardening was another way for them to get physical activity while also learning about science. With home-schooling, I realized that I could let my children learn through their interests. Just like my friend who went on to become a scientist because she spent so much time studying bugs and nature in the backyard, my kids could do the same. When children enjoy doing something, they make time for it and they engage in continual learning.

Of course, being called the happiest people in the world is a result of more than just parenting techniques, it is the culture using these techniques over generations of time. We can focus on the bits that are within our grasp. Danish society has so much that is a part of the "happiest people" title. Which I have explored in the book, "Nordic way of living: What makes them the happiest people on earth" Even if we can't fully replicate their culture, we can harness the contentment that comes from their parenting style and recreate some of the overall happiness Danish families have within our own families.

Summer Holiday

The entire nation of Denmark shuts down around July every summer. The citizens take what is called a "collective restoration," or in other words a group vacation (Sadeghi, 2021). This promotes the well-being of the country in the following ways:

- **Less pressure:** When everyone is taking time off work, there is no pressure to feel as though you're slacking and should be in the office. Therefore, it's easier for the Danish people to relax and enjoy themselves.

- **Quality time with the family:** The lack of stress and pressure means that you can focus 100% on your family and friends. You are literally and figuratively present in a way that isn't experienced in other cultures.

- **Cement the bonding process:** With no outside factors to take your attention away from family, you can learn more about the people you love. There are no distractions, and we all know how easy it is to lose focus and not retain information when distracted.

There are some things about Danish culture, especially within families, that I find appealing and also seem like they contribute to how this culture earns their "happiest people in the world" title. I want to finish up with a few parts of the culture that I have tried to incorporate into my own family.

For example, nobody is too good to do dishes, clear a table, or take out the trash. In Danish families, everyone takes a turn cooking and then cleaning up after a meal. Children are included in this practice. Without knowing about Danish parenting, this was something I tried to instill in my children when we began our special dinner nights. My husband and I didn't want our children to assume that just because I'm the mom meant I did the cooking and cleaning. By including them in the decision about the menu and then having them cook the meal themselves, they felt a sense of control. They were able to choose what we would eat for dinner and this helped when it came to meals that I cooked as well. They had started to gain an appreciation of what went into cooking every night for a family.

Communication was such a huge deal in our family and still is. If someone had a problem, we taught the kids to come together as a family to figure it out. No fighting or yelling was necessary. My husband and I were tired of all the bickering the kids did and we wanted to let them know that there were more mature, peaceful ways to solve a problem. Of course, with that, we had to teach them how to address their problems in a better manner than making accusatory statements.

Parenting the Danish way has improved our parenting. We have made more connections as a family along with finding a more effective way to handle family contention and decisions. We have stayed close. Overall, the best thing we could ask for as a parent is to have mentally and physically healthy children who have a great relationship with their parents, and that's what Danish parenting has given us.

Conclusion

Wrapping up the Magic of Parenting

Everyone is different and we each have unique ways of looking at and responding to the world. Within that difference, we all have lifestyles that, based on culture and environment, contribute to the way we live our life. Observing how other cultures raise their children can be fascinating, and with it comes insight and inspiration from the idea that maybe we could adopt some of their style into our own home.

I feel like when we see families practicing authentic communication it is the result of parenting in this manner. They don't let grievances fester, and by practicing empathy their relationships are stronger than before. Authentic communication would look like this:

- **Honesty:** Being truthful and avoiding deception.

- **Integrity:** Aligning your words with your actions.

- **Empathy:** Understanding and considering the perspective of others.

- **Self-awareness:** Recognizing your own thoughts, feelings, and behaviors.

- **Vulnerability:** Being willing to share your true self, even when it may be difficult.

Authentic communication can lead to stronger relationships, improved understanding, and increased trust. It's a valuable skill that can benefit you in both personal and professional settings. We have found doing this has been one of the best things we could have done for our family.

Overall, the Danish approach to parenting exemplifies a society that values cooperation, respect, and the well-being of its children while providing a nurturing and supportive environment for their growth and development. Danish parents:

- understand that children need that outdoor space and trust

- allow and encourage children to govern themselves

- communicate authentically

- promote confidence and humility

- teach children to find the best in every situation

- live and exemplify cozy contentment (hygge)

- spend quality time with their kids

- recognize that respect and trust are what foster the connection we all want in our parent-child relationships

Thank You

I appreciate that you have taken the time to research the idea of Danish parenting, but more than that, I sincerely hope you've taken away some ideas that will help you on the parenting journey. I mentioned extra parenting resources in Chapter 1, so I would like to list them here for you. I hope that you can take these resources along with what I've shared about the Danish parenting style to create your own magical style of parenting. This road my husband and I have been traveling doesn't have just one component of the journey; rather, it's a whole itinerary.

As you navigate your own parenting journey, check out

- Love and Logic Institute

- The Enneagram Test

- *The Child Whisperer* by Carol Tuttle

- Conscious Discipline Methodology

- *Leadership and Self Deception* by Arbinger Institute

As there are so many resources I could share, I'll have one more you could look out for to understand kids personality that I really like *Growing Kids with Character* by Hettie Brittz.

Please Let Me Know your Thoughts

Yes, we parent our own kids in our own way, but we learn from each other. That has been my goal with this book—to reach out to mothers and fathers, or soon-to-be parents—with what has helped me on the path. My family has managed to combine the various resources noted and have created something that we feel is quite magical.

I would love it if you would share your thoughts about what you have read and what your own parenting journey will look like once you start using Danish parenting techniques. You can do that by leaving a book review on Amazon. For any author, a review is the best compliment you can give. They also help others find the book.

To make it quick and easy for you scan the QR code with your camera, and it will take you straight to the review section.

Many thanks again for reading my book and please keep an eye out for our upcoming books in the *Wandering Lawtons Author Page on amazon*. My daughter has also published a book. A fashion coloring book of cutie girls with *60 fun, stylish hand drawn pictures and their stories*.

Our family has created memories, shared detours, and endured bad weather, but overall we are better than when we began. Parenting is not always a smooth journey, and some of the moments have not been so magical, but the ones that are and the relationship I have built with my kids is priceless.

I want to leave you with a poem by William Martin (1999), called "Do Not Ask Your Children to Strive," that comes to my mind when I think about *hygge* and *jante*:

"Do not ask your children

to strive for extraordinary lives.

Such striving may seem admirable,

but it is the way of foolishness.

Help them instead to find the wonder

and the marvel of an ordinary life.

Show them the joy of tasting

tomatoes, apples and pears.

Show them how to cry

when pets and people die.

Show them the infinite pleasure

in the touch of a hand.

And make the ordinary come alive for them.

The extraordinary will take care of itself."

-William Martin

Glossary

A*llemansrätten*: The right to roam. In Sweden, this concept is written into their constitution with the only restrictions being to stay off private or posted land. More importantly, however, it promotes the idea that access to nature is a right given to all, as long as nothing is destroyed and nobody is disturbed.

Fællesskab: Community, or togetherness. It is the feeling of belonging that comes from being part of a significant group.

Friluftsliv: No matter the weather, it's the chance to go outside and enjoy nature. A loose translation would be "open-air life."

Hygge: A sense of coziness that leads to contentment and well-being, or an intentional intimacy that promotes safety, balance, and harmony with those around you. A concept integral to the Danish sense of well-being.

Janteloven: (yanteh-loven), also known as the Law of Jante. Originating as a satirical concept in Danish literature, Janteloven is traditionally seen as a critical lens on a societal tendency to prioritize community over individuality, often discouraging self-promotion and standing out.

Kos: A state of mind that indicates calmness, being present in the moment, deep well-being, and contentment. It can be experienced alone or with others.

Lagom: A behavior that is not too much, but not too little. It is a way to have a balanced compromise without controversial discussions or interactions.

Stör inte, förstör inte: Common-sense conduct in nature, or literally, "don't disturb, don't destroy." Children in countries like Denmark are taught this concept from the time they can walk, and it's even taught in school.

Trivsel: Thriving or well-being. This is something that educators in Danish culture focus on since they believe that academic skills will come with a strong sense of well-being.

References

Alexander, J. J., & Andersson, C. S. (2022, February 15). *Fællesskab and belonging*. Othering & Belonging Institute. https://belonging.berke ley.edu/democracy-belonging-forum/papers/faellesskab

Altman, A. (2016, December 18). The year of hygge, the Danish obsession with getting cozy. *The New Yorker*. https://www.newyorker.com/culture/culture-desk/the-year-of-hygge-the-d anish-obsession-with-getting-cozy#:~:text=It%20derives%20from%20a%20 sixteenth

Arnold, K. (2022, May 12). *What Sweden teaches us about parenting and the outdoors*. Outside Online. https://www.outsideonline.com/culture/acti ve-families/what-sweden-can-teach-us-about-outdoor-parenting/

Auxier, B., Anderson, M., Perrin, A., and Turner, E. (2020, July 2 8). *Parenting children in the age of screens*. Pew Research Cen- ter. https://www.pewresearch.org/internet/2020/07/28/parenting-childre n-in-the-age-of-screens/

Bardoloi, Y. (2018, March 1). *What is the OECD, and what does it do?* Young Post. https://www.scmp.com/yp/discover/your-voice/opinion/artic le/3070213/what-oecd-and-what-does-it-do

Brady, S. (2020, October 1). *Embrace winter like a Norwegian this year by practising 'friluftsliv.'* Lonely Planet. https://www.lonelyplanet.com/news/what-is-friluftsliv

Bryant, C. D. (n.d.). *What is respect? Definition for kids.* Talking with Trees. https://talkingtreebooks.com/teaching-resources-catalog/definitions/what-is-respect.html

Cepeda, M. (2016, August 4). 5 simple steps to raising a well-behaved child while disciplining less. *Woman's Day.* https://www.womansday.com/relationships/family-friends/advice/a55862/child-whisperer-infographic/

Cherry, K. (2023a, May 24). *What autonomy means in psychology.* Verywell Mind. https://www.verywellmind.com/autonomy-in-psychology-how-to-make-your-own-choices-7496882?

Cherry, K. (2023b, July 5). *Do you have an authoritative parenting style?* Verywell Mind. https://verywellmind.com/what-is-authoritative-parenting-2794956

Christensen, J. (2021, May 28). *Children and screen time: How much is too much?* Mayo Clinic Health System. https://www.mayoclinichealthsystem.org/hometown-health/speaking-of-health/children-and-screen-time

Christian, H. (2023, September 18). *Time to go out and play.* The UNESCO Courier. https://courier.unesco.org/en/articles/time-go-out-and-play

Cline, F., & Fay, J. (2006). *Parenting with love and logic: Teaching children responsibility.* Navpress.

Conscious discipline methodology. (n.d.). Conscious Discipline. https://consciousdiscipline.com/methodology/

The Danish way of parenting: Summary & review. (2020, April 29). Perfectionist Mom. https://www.perfectionistmom.com/the-danish-way-of-parenting-summary-review/#:~:text=The%20parenting%20style%20used%20in

Erickson, D. (2023, September 25). *Scandinavian minimalism: A comprehensive guide.* HipDiggs. https://www.hipdiggs.com/scandinavian-minimalism/

Fay, J., & Fay, C. (n.d.). *Parenting with love & logic.* Love and Logic Institute. https://aae.lewiscenter.org/documents/AAE/Love%20and%20Logic/Parenting/Parentingwithlandl.pdf

Glassy, D., & Tandon, P. (2022, April 28). *Playing outside: Why it's important for kids.* HealthyChildren.org . https://www.healthychildren.org/English/family-life/power-of-play/Pages /playing-outside-why-its-important-for-kids.aspx

Gray, A. (2017, March 17). *Denmark has the best work-life balance. Here's why.* World Economic Forum. https://www.weforum.org/agenda/2017/03/ denmark-best-work-life-balance-oecd/

Helweg-Larsen, M. (2018, March 20). *Why Denmark dominates the World Happiness Report rankings year after year.* The Conversation. https://theconversation.com/why-denmark-dominates-the-world-hap piness-report-rankings-year-after-year-93542

Hortop, A. (2019). Harnessing the Scandinavian concepts of "lagom" and "hygge" in creative bliss. *British Journal of Occupational Therapy, 82*(8), 24. https://www.rcot.co.uk/sites/default/files/Session%2037.1%20-%20Harness ing%20Scandinavian%20concepts%20of%20lagom%20and%20hygge.pdf

Hygge. (n.d.). Tips@Home. https://view.ceros.com/john-l-scott/tip21/p/1

King James Bible. (2024). King James Bible Online. https://www.kingjam esbibleonline.org (Original work published 1769)

Koons, A. (2019, October 21). *T.H.I.N.K. before you speak.* HSL-DA. https://hslda.org/post/think-before-you-speak#:~:text=T%20%E2%80 %93%20Is%20what%20I

"Kos" is Norwegian for having a good time. (n.d.). Visit Norway. https:// www.visitnorway.com/typically-norwegian/kos-means-having-a-good-time/

Leadership and self-deception overview. (n.d.). Arbinger Institute. https:// hub.arbinger.com/home/leadership-and-self-deception-overview

Luxton, E. (2016, March 4). *Does working fewer hours make you more productive?* World Economic Forum. https://www.weforum.org/agenda/20 16/03/does-working-fewer-hours-make-you-more-productive/

Markham, L. (2017). *How do children learn right from wrong?* Psychology Today. https://www.psychologytoday.com/us/blog/peaceful-parents-happy -kids/201703/how-do-children-learn-right-wrong

Martin, W. (1999). *The Parent's Tao Te Ching: Ancient Advice for Modern Parents.* Da Capo Lifelong Books.

Maternity leave and paternity leave when working in Denmark. (2024). Ø r e s u n d d i r e k t . https://www.oresunddirekt.se/en/working-in-denmark/family-and-parenting/p arental-leave-when-working-in-denmark#:~:text=In%20total%2C%20parents% 20in%20Denmark%20get%2052%20weeks

McGurk, L. A. (2020). *There's no such thing as bad weather: A Scandinavian mom's secrets for raising healthy, resilient, and confident kids (from friluftsliv to-hygge).* Touchstone.

Mellish, K. X. (2019, January 6). *Tips for living with a Danish family.* How to Live in Denmark. https://www.howtoliveindenmark.com/stories-about-life-in -denmark/living-with-a-danish-family-2/

Merriam-Webster. (n.d.-a). Essence. In *Merriam-Webster.com dictionary.* Retrieved December 23, 2023, from https://www.merriam-webster.com/dictiona ry/essence#:~:text=Kids%20Definition-

Merriam-Webster. (n.d.-b). Respect. In *Merriam-Webster.com dictionary.* Retrieved December 23, 2023 from https://www.merriam-webster.com/dictionar y/respect

Ministry of Foreign Affairs of Denmark. (2018). *Lifelong education.* Denma rk.dk. https://denmark.dk/society-and-business/lifelong-education

OECD. (2022). *Denmark.* Education GPS. https://gpseducation.oecd.org/ CountryProfile?primaryCountry=DNK&treshold=10&topic=PI

Quiz. (n.d.). Enneagram Test. https://enneagramtest.com/quiz?afid=msens &msclkid=c7788d0d7ec91fe97b65e8dbd445deda

Risman, B. J. (2020, December 6). *Is Denmark a feminist utopia?* Psychology Today. https://www.psychologytoday.com/us/blog/gender-questions/202012 /is-denmark-feminist-utopia

Rush, T., & Burgess, L. (2023, November 22). *Left brain vs. right brain: Fact and fiction.* MedicalNewsToday. https://www.medicalnewstoday.com/articles/ 321037#functions-of-each-hemisphere

Russell, H. (2016, April 11). *The Danish way of life: Putting loved ones first.* Stylist. https://www.stylist.co.uk/life/why-family-matters-in-denmark-hap piness-loved-ones-learning-people-friends-people-values/63915

Sadeghi, M. (2021, January 2). Fact check: Denmark is among world's happiest countries, but it's not no. 1. *USA TO-DAY.* https://www.usatoday.com/story/news/factcheck/2021/01/02/fact -check-denmark-among-happiest-countries-but-isnt-no-1/4107107001/

Sanvictores, T., & Mendez, M. D. (2022, September 18). *Types of parenting styles and effects on children.* StatPearls Publishing. https://www.ncbi.nlm. nih.gov/books/NBK568743/

Sheldrake, R., Amos, R., & Reiss, M. (2019). *Children and nature: A research evaluation for The Wildlife Trusts.* The Wildlife Trusts. https://www.wildlifetrusts.org/sites/default/files/2019-11/Children%20an d%20Nature%20-%20UCL%20and%20The%20Wildlife%20Trusts%20Full %20Report.pdf

Siegel, D. J., & Bryson, T. P. (2011). *The whole-brain child.* Delacorte Press.

Scandinavian mentality. (n.d.). ConsultingCheck. https://www.consult ingcheck.com/en/topics/scandinavian-mentality

Sørensen, M. C., Andersen, R. N., Schmidt, S., Jensen, J. B., Brix, J., Limskov, N., Christiansen, S., Jakobsen, J. K. S., Jørgensen, K. A., Lucacel, R., & Jensen, H. (2022). *Practitioner change journeys: a mixed-methods study of play facilitation in Danish daycare.* The Lego Foundation. https://doi.o rg/10.13140/RG.2.2.16749.26083

Spending time in nature can improve children's confidence. (2019, November 7). UCL News. https://www.ucl.ac.uk/news/2019/nov/spending-time -nature-can-improve-childrens-confidence

Tuttle, C. (2012). *The child whisperer: The ultimate handbook for raising happy, successful, cooperative children.* Live Your Truth Press.

Understanding the law of jante (janteloven). (n.d.). Living With Norwegians. https://livingwithnorwegians.com/understanding-the-law-of-jante-j anteloven/

Walsh, E., & Walsh, D. (2019, May 9). *How children develop empathy.* Psychology Today. https://www.psychologytoday.com/us/blog/smart-parenting-smarter-kids/201905/how-children-develop-empathy

What is the education system like in Denmark? (n.d.). Elab Education Laboratory. https://elabedu.eu/education-system/what-is-the-education-system-like-in-denmark/

Whitebread, D., Basilio, M., Kuvalja, M., & Verma, M. (2012, April). The importance of play. *Toy Industries of Europe.* https://www.waldorf-resources.org/fileadmin/files/pictures/Early_Childhood/dr_david_whitebread_-_the_importance_of_play.pdf

Winther-Lindqvist, D. A. (2016, October 22). The role of play in Danish child care. In C. Ringsmose & G. Kragh-Müller (Eds.), *Nordic Social Pedagogical Approach to Early Years* (pp. 95–114). https://doi.org/10.1007/978-3-319-42557-3_6

Wiking, M. (2016). *The little book of hygge: The Danish way to live well.* Penguin Random House.

Work-life balance. (n.d.). Denmark.dk. https://denmark.dk/society-and-business/work-life-balance

Work-life balance. (2014). OECD Better Life Index. https://www.oecdbetterlifeindex.org/topics/work-life-balance/

World Economic Forum. (2022, July 13). *Global gender gap report 2022.* http://weforum.org/reports/global-gender-gap-report-2022/

World Happiness Report. (2023, March 20). *World happiness, trust and social connections in times of crisis.* https://worldhappiness.report/ed/2023/world-happiness-trust-and-social-connections-in-times-of-crisis/#ranking-of-happiness-2020-2022

World Health Organization. (2019, April 24). *To grow up healthy, children need to sit less and play more.* https://www.who.int/news/item/24-04-2019-to-grow-up-healthy-children-need-to-sit-less-and-play-more yapbeelee. (2023, July 20). *Positive and negative impacts of electronic devices on children.* We Have Kids. https://wehavekids.com/parenting/dlectronic-devices-and-gadgets-to-Children

Zeltser, F. (2021, October 5). *Here's what makes "authoritative parents" different from the rest—and why psychologists say it's the best parenting style.* CNBC. https://www.cnbc.com/2021/10/05/child-psychologist-explains-why-authoritative-parenting-is-the-best-style-for-raising-smart-confident-kids.html

Zosh, J., Caudreau, C., Golinkoff, R. M., & Hirsh-Pasek, K. (2022). The power of playful learning in the early childhood setting. *Young Children, 77*(2). https://www.naeyc.org/resources/pubs/yc/summer2022/power-playful-learning

Martin, W. (n.d.). Do not ask your children to strive for extraordinary lives. Goodreads. https://www.goodreads.com/quotes/505843-do-not-ask-your-children-to-strive-for-extraordinary-lives

∞

The Wandering Lawtons

Our Family Books & YouTube Channel:

Hi there! We're the Lawton's, and we love to explore and discover the world around us. After several years of homeschooling, field trips, and travel, we decided it was time to share our adventures with others. While life isn't always sunshine and rainbows, we feel incredibly blessed to have the opportunity to wander, learn, and grow together. Our family's explorations have become something we want to capture and remember forever, and we're excited to invite you along on this journey.

Our amazing kids also love being part of the process! My daughter, at just seven years old, has already published her first coloring book, *Fashion Coloring Book: 60 Fun Stylish Hand-Drawn Cute Girls & Their Stories*. If you love family fun and the thrill of discovery, come follow along with us as we explore, create, and make memories that last a lifetime.

To make it easier to find our daughters book scan this QR code:

To see our YouTube Channel view the QR code through your devises camera.

Happy Wanderings! Now Lets Get to It!

More Books From the Publisher

Giving Tree Press is a dynamic collective of authors and editors who have come together to create a space to share their own unique background and perspective. Our diverse team includes educators, travelers, artist, mentors, Christians, and parents who bring their wealth of knowledge and experience to the table.

Experience and Expertise

We draw from extensive research and a deep understanding of the respective fields, and we are passionate about creating content that resonates with our readers and fosters a sense of connection. With every page turned, you'll find yourself immersed in the rich narratives crafted by Giving Tree Press's talented team. Their unique blend of expertise confirms that each book offers something for everyone - from practical tips for everyday challenges to captivating tales that whisk you away on an adventure.

Our Goal

ORM

Our goal is to bring individuals words to life in their dream to publish. These books are not just to tell but also to inspire, whether it's helping parents navigate the challenges of raising children, guiding young people on their path to adulthood, find mindfulness and relaxation or transporting readers to fascinating places and/or periods in history.

At Giving Tree Press we believe in the power of words to inspire thought-provoking ideas and encourage self-reflection. Our mission is to create content that not only entertains but also enriches the lives of our readers. Do you have a book in your heart, you have desired to be published? Reach out we can help!

View the QR code to visit our catalog of great books and authors.

Our popular teen book is by Emily C. Fox *Leadership for Teens: 25 Key Life Skills Everyone Should Master*. Which is also penned by A. Lawton under her pen name.

Scan this QR code to join our community of readers who love discovering new stories and **supporting independent authors**. Your positive, honest **reviews on Amazon help** increase our authors' credibility and visibility. By subscribing, you'll **get exclusive updates** on our latest releases and be the first to know when our **E-books are on sale or available for free.**

www.ingramcontent.com/pod-product-compliance
Lightning Source LLC
LaVergne TN
LVHW051416080426
835508LV00022B/3117